DATE DUE

GAYLORD		PRINTED IN U.S.A.

EVALUATION OF ADOPTION POLICY AND PRACTICE

J. P. TRISELIOTIS

FOREWORD

MEGAN BROWNE, M.B.E., B.A.

Senior Lecturer, Department of Social Administration, Edinburgh University

EDINBURGH 1970

TO   VIVIENNE

FOREWORD

by Megan Browne, M.B.E., B.A., Senior
Lecturer, Department of Social Administration, University of Edinburgh.

This review of events at the various stages in the process
of child adoption in Scotland in the year 1965, is a version
of a Ph.D. thesis, much reduced in size, and therefore in
detail. It presents in summarized form the research findings
from an enquiry carried out at a significant point in time by
someone particularly well qualified for the task.

In 1967 an Act of Sederunt made it possible for the first
time to obtain access to court records of adoptions, and Dr.
Triseliotis speedily appreciated the opportunity this presented to follow a sizeable number of adoptions through all the
stages which this process involves. Previously research had
been hampered not only by the very multiplicity of these
processes, but also by the effect of the secrecy, particularly
regarding the deliberations and decision making of the Court,
which, however necessary to maintain privacy and confidentiality in the individual case, had hitherto defeated attempts
to thread the various episodes in the sequence together.

The possibility of this linkage had to exist before the
full significance of each episode could be estimated, but
feasibility alone would not have sufficed to increase our
understanding if the person carrying out the research had
not had particular training and experience.

Dr. Triseliotis trained as a social caseworker, and has
had wide experience in the children's field of such work,
with both normal and deviant populations. He was thus in a
particularly favourable position for the appraisal, since he
had already formulated a number of queries and hypotheses
about adoption processes which were ready to be explored and
tested.

The task confronting him demanded both energy and in-
dustry; these he possessed – but in addition his particular
background enabled him to extract the full meaning from the
mass of material elicited. The methods Dr. Triseliotis employed have included appraisal of the social worker's part
in the adoption process by employing the touchstone of
social work principles, and knowledge of human growth and
behaviour, in its evaluation. At the same time he demon-
strates that the functions of the Sheriff in this situation
cannot be fully exercised unless sufficient evidence is
presented to him, and this focusses attention on certain
ambiguities in the role of the Curator ad Litem, as well as
on the use of pro forma reports by social workers. One of
the more striking facts to emerge is the distressing tend-
ancy for well-intentioned people at many stages of this

process to abrogate full responsibility, believing that it will either have already been exercised at an earlier stage, or that all will be put right at some subsequent time.

Evaluation of the practices of agencies arranging adoptions whether statutory or voluntary was undertaken and here Dr. Triseliotis's material suggests that we should re-consider the validity of certain practices in adoption work, which, however carefully thought out in principle, may operate in a negative sense if they become stereotyped, and thus fail to be related to the particular circumstances of the case. This tends to occur, for example, in relation to policies which place undue reliance on the possibility of "matching" adopted child and adopters; or in relation to policies which result in making a pre-adoption placement of the child an invariable rule. Dr. Triseliotis also suggests that clarification by an adoption agency of the grounds for the "rejection" of potential adopters is overdue. There is evidence that this is too often related simply to supply and demand in a particular agency's area and clientele, rather than to the facts of the situation in the wider community, and that potential adopters may be being discouraged from applying when there are children, particularly older children, who are available for adoption.

The material Dr. Triseliotis presents will have significance for many people. Fellow social workers in the field of adoption practice, not only in Scotland, but in the whole of the U.K. and overseas, wherever adoption is an accepted way of creating new family units, will find much to stimulate re-thinking of their present policies, besides suggestions for the creation of new policies. The material will also shed new light on social work factors in the adoption situation which should be of interest to those in allied disciplines particularly in medicine and law. It could be that consideration of this material may lead practitioners of whatever discipline to find ways in which to work more closely together in this most searching, yet ultimately most rewarding field.

ACKNOWLEDGEMENTS

This study would not have been possible without the co-operation of many individuals and organizations. I would like to take this opportunity to express my real gratitude to them all.

I owe many thanks to the staff and administrative personnel of the Scottish Education Department (Social Work Services Group), for assisting me to obtain access to the records of the Courts and of the children's departments. Special thanks are due to the Clerks of the twenty Sheriff Courts, the Chief Officers of the eight children's departments, and the Directors of the four voluntary Adoption Societies which participated in the study, as well as to the great numbers of caseworkers and Court officials for their most willing and encouraging help.

Much gratitude is due to Janet Lusk, the Director of the Guild of Service and to Pam Andrews, Head Medical Social Worker at the Royal Infirmary and to their staff for their continuous support and co-operation.

My thanks are also due to the administrators of the Moray Endowment Fund and to Edinburgh University for allocating research grants that helped to get the study off the ground. Special thanks are extended also to the administrative personnel of the Social Work Services Group and the Trustees of The Carnegie Trust for the Universities of Scotland for making funds available to make this publication possible.

Finally, I am greatly indebted to my two advisors for the study, Miss Megan Browne and Professor Forfar, who not only gave generously of their time, but also offered constructive advise and guidance throughout this research.

T A B L E S

C O N T E N T S

CHAPTER ONE

HISTORICAL <u>BACKGROUND TO CURRENT ADOPTION</u> PRACTICES

> "Whereas originally the aim of adoption was
> essentially to provide the adopters with
> direct heirs, it is now increasingly
> considered as a unique means of providing
> a permanent parental relationship for
> children deprived of their natural
> parents". (United Nations, "Study on the
> Adoption of Children")

Before 1926, adoption, in the sense of the permanent
transfer of parental rights and duties in respect of a child
to another person, and their assumption by him, was unknown
in British law.   Until then, the rights, liabilities and
duties of natural parents were inalienable.   Previously
there had been informal arrangements by which families
brought up children, mostly from within their own kinship
circle and occasionally from without, but the practice
offered no security to any of the parties involved.   Current
adoption legislation aims at regulating the relationship
between natural and adopting families, mostly childless ones,
and protecting the child's interests.   Since its inception,
the original Act has been amended and overhauled on several
occasions and at the time of writing the comprehensive Act
of 1958 is in the process of being changed to give expression to new ideas gained in the course of practice and
the administration of the law.

Adoption was practised in the ancient Eastern civil-
isations, and traces of the custom can be found in the
literature of these countries.   The practice reflected
aspects of the goal system of the societies in which it was
followed.   Such goals were connected with the need for an
heir, or for acquiring fame, or with the duty of perpet-
uating the domestic worship.   Sargon, the founder of Babylon,
Oedipus, who later became king of Thebes, and Moses were
reared outside their own families.   From Genesis, we also
learn that at one time barren wives were giving their
husbands their female slaves with a view to adopting any
children born of this association.   Among the Hindus,
adoption is recorded in the most ancient legal code and is
discussed in Sanskrit commentaries.   In Greece, Solon introduced in 594 B.C. laws regulating and sanctioning adoption in
order that a family might not die out.   Isaeus,[1] an Athenian
orator who lived around 400 B.C., defended before the courts
the claims of many adopted sons for the estates of their
adoptive families. (The Greek word 'hyiothesia' means the
adoption of boys.) Under Roman law, the position of children
was carefully secured and the birth of subsequent legitimate

children did not deprive adopted ones of their rights. Both
the Greek and Roman systems, however, had as their primary
motive the continuity of the adopter's family and not succour
for unwanted children. The first departure, from the old concept of adoption being practised in the interests of the
adopters, was introduced by the creators of the "great code"
of Alphonso X of Castille in 1300 A.D. This code gave consideration to the welfare of the child, by providing some
measure of protection for it. Margaret Mead [2] in her more
recent studies of primitive societies describes how, in many
of the tropical Islands she visited, the custom exists of
families exchanging babies for rearing outside the family.
The custom is an example of the more 'open' type of family
life of these societies compared to that where there are more
closely-knit families, who mainly adopt from within their kinship circle. In many other cultures such as the W. Indies,
formal adoption until recently was found unnecessary because
traditionally the child, orphan or illegitimate, was accepted
into the circle of the extended family.

Some form of adoption appears to have been practised in
Britain during the pre-reformation period, though there is no
evidence to suggest that the practice was either widespread or
connected with the welfare of children. The Oxford Dictionary
traces adoption and its cognates back to the fourteenth
century and Marbeck in his 'book notes' of 1581, wrote: "The
lawiers define adoption to be a legitimate act imitating
nature, found out for their solace and comfort which have no
children". Shakespeare refers to adoption in Richard II;IV,i
and pursues the subject in Henry VI,I,i. In an exchange
between Warwick and Exeter, the latter's comments amount to
saying that it is not possible to substitute an outsider, for
a rightful heir. This attitude towards property and inheritance is one of the factors that appears to have exercised
considerable influence in delaying adoption legislation in
Britain.

The Relationship Between Illegitimacy, the Boarding-Out System and Adoption.

The use of adoption as a means of dealing with the
problem of illegitimacy appears to be of more recent origin
than the practice of adoption itself. Adoption in the modern
sense is practised as an emergency measure to deal with the
problems of illegitimacy and childlessness. Prior to the
introduction of marriage and especially of monogamy (as
distinct from tribal and religious marital rites), the dis-
tinction between legitimate and illegitimate was somewhat
blurred. It is difficult to trace how and when illegitimate children came increasingly to be regarded as outcasts of
society. In England the origin of their "persecution" goes
back to the 8th century, but it was with the reformation and
the emergence of a Puritan outlook with its adherence to a
strict moral code that an attitude of hostility and severe
condemnation came to be attached to illegitimacy. Social

stigma became associated with illegitimacy and gave rise to persecutions and punishment. The community in its earnestness to punish the "offending" parents, forgot the needs of the children. Crammond[3] in his treatise on 'Illegitimacy in Banffshire' describes how as recently as 1748, "men and also women for their immoralities were scourged through the streets of the burghs by the common hangman and frequently banished from the town ..". In the case of aggravated offences men and women had to stand at the church door "bair footit and bair leggit for the space of one yeir". In 1552 Christ's Hospital tried to provide for abandoned children, but by the middle of the 17th century it had become reputable and would only accept legitimate ones. The grant that Thomas Coram received from public funds, to enable him to open Britain's first foundling hospital, was attacked on the grounds that it was likely to increase the evil he was seeking to remedy. Similarly it was only at the beginning of this century that Dr. Barnardo's agreed to accept illegitimate children within their Homes, previously refusing to do so for fear of encouraging illegitimacy. Moral, economic, social, demographic and religious factors have all played their part in shaping community attitudes toward the unmarried mother and the illegitimate child.

From an examination of various documents of the 18th century, no evidence was found to suggest any special public sympathy towards the deserted or illegitimate child that could have led to his adoption. The Foundling Hospital which was started in London in 1739 with the object of accepting mainly illegitimate children, unwanted or deserted by their parents, records the first adoption of a child as late as 1802 and this appeared to be an isolated occurrence. Glasgow Town Hospital which initiated a similar system in 1733 has no record of placing children for de facto adoption, other than on a fostering basis. Further evidence confirming the absence and almost ignorance of the practice of adoption in Britain before the 19th century, comes from the letters of Lady Montagu.[4] In 1718 whilst staying in Constantinople, she wrote to a friend in England extolling the custom of adoption among the Greeks and Armenians of the City and wondering why it could not be copied in Britain. Isolated cases of adoption, mostly by relatives, came to notice during the first half of the 19th century. Gerin[5] in her biography of Charlotte Brontë, writes that the Hudsons with whom Miss Brontë stayed, had been married in 1830 but were childless. At the time of Miss Brontes visit they had staying with them a seven year old niece of Mrs. Hudson "who they later adopted". George Eliot[6] in her novel 'Silas Marner' remarks that "adoption was more remote from the ideas and habits of that time". Nancy, one of the characters in the novel later says to her husband when expressing fears that an adopted child may not turn out well: "Don't you remember what that lady we met at the Royston Baths told us about the child her sister adopted? That was the only adopting I ever heard of: and the child was transported when it was twenty-three".

A marked increase of de facto adoptions became evident after the middle of the last century and was mainly an off-shoot of the boarding-out system and of the practice of 'baby farming'. The boarding-out of deprived children in Scotland spread mainly after the 1830's though there were still acute differences of opinion among the various parishes concerning its relative merit. Anderson [7] writing in 1870 after his personal inspection of 320 boarded-out children in the Edinburgh area and the borders, concluded that the scheme was the nearest approach to the family circle that the circumstances admit of. In Scotland, unlike England, the principle of "less eligibility", following the 1834 Poor Law Act, was only sparsely applied as the building of institutions would have been too costly for many of the smaller authorities. For similar reasons many parochial Boards encouraged the boarding-out of deprived children. This Policy discouraged the setting-up of big training institutions which by the 1860's were springing up in England. The Paisley Board of Guardians in a report in 1866 [8] added in support of the boarding-out system: "We believe that children brought up in public institutions, when at length turned out into the world, are, as a general rule, feeble in body and mind, and less able to fight their way through life than those who come from the common walks of life". By 1870 the returns of some of the Scottish Parishes show that some of the children boarded-out were adopted, mostly by their foster-parents but occasionally by strangers too. The adopted children were mostly orphans or children deserted by their parents. In an apparent effort to encourage the adoption of children whose parents were alive but had deserted, the Inspector of Barony Parish suggested withholding information to anyone about the child's where-abouts to prevent parents or others from interfering with the child and the adopters.

Along with the development of the boarding-out system, the second half of the nineteenth century saw the rapid spread of baby farming i.e. the private rearing, mostly of illegitimate children, for a premium. The evils of this practice were revealed at the notorious trial of Margaret Waters and Sarah Ellis and led to the appointment of a Select Committee in 1870 to report on "Infant Life Protection". [9] Some of the witnesses told the Committee that in all parts of London, Edinburgh and Glasgow there were a large number of private houses used as lying-in establishments where unmarried women were confined. When the infants were born, some of them were taken away by their mothers, but if they were to be "adopted", as was usually the practice, the owner of the establishment received for the "adoption" a lump sum of money which ranged from £5 to £100 according to the means of the woman who was confined. The infant was then immediately removed "to the worst class of baby farming houses" where there was every inducement to get rid of the baby, unless the mother was likely to come back to look for it, which she seldom did. These children were put out for

reward with the deliberate knowledge, and, probably, also with
the deliberate intention that they would be sure to die very
quickly. There was, however, a smaller group of children who
were genuine 'de facto' adoption cases. Most unmarried mothers
resorted to baby-farming of this type, mainly as a result of
the increasing stigma attached to illegitimacy during the
second half of the last century and because of the social
burden of bringing up an illegitimate child. (Children were
less valuable by then as the Factory Acts put an end to child
labour.) Philanthropists and charitable organisations were at
the time afraid to touch the problem of illegitimacy for fear
of being seen as encouraging immorality.

The passing of the Births and Deaths Registration Act of
1874 went some way to contribute to the eradication of the
anonymous destruction of infants born in unregistered
maternity homes. It was not, however, till 1911 that the
Parish Council of Glasgow was told by one of its committees
that "nearly for a year now they had no case of baby-farming
in its worst form and that it was practically now extinct".[10]
The Council attributed their success to an arrangement with
the newspapers to refuse adoption advertisements. The Council
was told that in the County of Lanark a mother and her
daughter obtained, through press adverts, some 25 babies at a
premium, within a year; some subsequently died or disappeared. The report made the point, however, that some
people were genuinely interested in adopting infants and the
majority were 'adopted' without any money payments usually a
few hours after the child's birth.

From the last quarter of the 19th century onwards
adoption came to be seen mainly as a means of dealing with
the problem of illegitimacy, but up to the end of the Second
World War the practice was chiefly confined to the working
classes. The work of Josephine Butler towards the end of
the last century, marked the beginning of a slightly softer
attitude towards the unmarried mother and her child but this
was found in a very small section of the community. A re-
examination of attitudes was made inevitable during the first
Warld War when illegitimacy suddenly increased, mainly as a
result of the movement of troops and the unsettled conditions prevailing. Great interest was aroused as a result
of a letter on the subject that appeared in the Morning Post
of May 2nd 1915, contributed by Mr. McNeil M.P. He argued
for positive provision by the State for these illegitimate
children and for sympathy for their mothers. He urged the
casting aside of established theories, prejudices and
formulas about "setting a premium on immorality". For the
next few weeks a great number of letters continued appear-
ing in the 'Morning Post' and the 'Daily Mail'. However,
in this correspondence the needs of the children were lost
sight of and most of the writers focussed on the moral
issues, especially on condemning the mothers, with little
or no responsibility being attributed to the fathers, the
latter being seen as war heroes. The Archbishop of

Canterbury wrote: "There can be nothing more cruel, either as regards the soldiers or as regards unmarried women who are likely to become mothers, than that we should at this moment seem in the slightest degree to be sweeping aside the values which ordinarily govern us in everyday life". The Mothers' League – a voluntary body – urged the rich with few children "to come forward and help to save and rear the babies we want so badly". Good provisions for the child were being advocated mainly on population grounds. It was argued that the tremendous toll of able-bodied men at the front called for replacements and that one way of doing this was by taking especial care of illegitimate children because of the high mortality rates amongst them. Unmarried mothers were grouped into 'desirable' and 'undesirable' ones. The 'desirable' ones who deserved help and sympathy were those stably co-habiting and those who had been courting for some time. To these, no encouragement should be given to get rid of the baby through adoption or otherwise. The keeping of the baby, it was argued, would help the mothers stay 'chaste'. The 'undesirable' ones were described as careless, frivolous, indiscreet, vicious and drunken. It was urged that the children should be separated from these mothers and be placed in institutions where their identity would be lost and they could grow up probably honest and good citizens. It was also suggested that foster and adoptive parents should be found to undertake to look after them and bring them up as their own children.[11] A few 'wealthy' and 'titled' ladies adopted children who were orphaned because of the war, but there is no evidence to suggest that this practice spread to any appreciable degree.

At the start of the present century a number of Church organisations and some independent ones, like the 'Mother's League', began to form Moral Welfare Societies and to open Mother and Baby Homes for single mothers. In Glasgow, a Home for Deserted Mothers was established in 1875, but admission was allowed only to those who were mothers for the first time. In Edinburgh, the Lauriston Home for Unmarried Mothers was established in 1899 "to provide temporary shelter for young unmarried girls about to be mothers for the first time". This last rule was not removed till 1966. The Salvation Army opened its own Home in Edinburgh in 1912. Community attitudes and social pressures, often punitive ones, reflected themselves in some of the rules and requirements that governed the running of a number of Mother and Baby Homes.

Greater tolerance and compassion towards the unmarried mother and her child was considerably promoted by the work of the National Council for the Unmarried Mother and her Child which was formed in 1918. Public opinion seems to have moved in a more liberal direction after the first World War but Browne[14] sees 1945 as the year that marks the beginning of a general move towards a more liberal climate on this subject. There is much that suggests that

this change gradually came about through increased opportunities to study the subject of illegitimacy and that those
in turn were made possible through an increase in the amount
of factual material made available since 1945. This was
the first year in which questions about unmarried mothers and
illegitimate babies were included in the annual returns which
local welfare authorities were required to submit to the
Mininister of Health. The assembling of facts was a step towards dispelling prejudice and permitting a more rational
view to be taken. It is also probable that present-day young
people have different attitudes to the matter compared to
their parents. Sex as a subject appears to be more freely
discussed among the young people of today. Hamilton,[15]
however, expresses a less optimistic view when she says:
"From the social point of view we are not certain where we
stand". She adds that "destructive social attitudes and inadequate social measures are often ignored which could more
fairly be charged with being the source of infanticide,
abortion, still-birth and other calamities, than the simple
fact of illegitimate conception". At present, economic factors very often combine with social and emotional forces to
make an unmarried mother give up her child for adoption.
Because of this, warnings are very appropriately being given,
that the needs of the unmarried mother should not be tailored
to the needs and practice of adoption.

Serious pressure for the introduction of adoption legislation increased after the end of the first Warld War.
Public opinion appeared readier then to consider the introduction of legislation to regulate the position of many
children who were in a de facto adoption situation. As the
first voluntary adoption workers and the agency committees
began to gain some experience of adoption work, they became
more aware of the drawbacks of "de facto" adoption and they
started campaigning for the introduction of suitable legislation. The arrangements that existed then offered no protection either to the child or to the adoptive parents or
for that matter to the natural parents. Adoptive parents
had no guarantee that the child would not be reclaimed by
its natural parents and likewise the natural parents had
no guarantee that the child would have a secure home or
that they would not be asked to take it back. Under pressure both from within and from outside the House, the
Government appointed a committee with Sir Alfred
Hopkinson, K.C. as Chairman "to consider the desirability
of making legal provision for adoption and the form any
such provision should take". [12]

The Hopkinson Committee reported in 1921 and it came
out strongly in favour of adoption legislation.[12] The
Committee felt that it was better to place children with
families for adoption than in an institution with a number
of others. It referred to the increase of adoptions during
and after the war and said that there was evidence that the
practice of adoption without definite legal sanction had

been accompanied in many cases by serious evils. A private member's Bill was introduced in 1922 but had to be abandoned on the dissolution of Parliament, after reaching the report stage. There was considerable disagreement among members of the House whether such legislation was necessary at all. Under further pressure the Government of the day appointed a new committee in 1924 with Mr. Justice Tomlin as its chairman.[13] The Committee reported within a year but it was very cautious in its comments when assessing the need for adoption legislation. The Committee remarked that they were unable to ascertain the demand for such legislation. Contrary to the views expressed by the Hopkinson Committee, the Tomlison Committee saw the increase in adoptions as the result of the 1914-18 war and did not think that this interest would be maintained. The Committee's view, however, that adoption by itself could not resolve the problem of the unwanted child, "especially the older one", was as true then as it is today. The Committee followed their first report with a second and third one but in spite of their reservations a draft Bill was submitted to Parliament and it formed the basis of the 1926 Adoption Act, (1930 for Scotland). In the debate that followed in the House, the discussion was focussed on how to promote the interests of children, adoptive parents and natural parents as well.

Adoption Legislation

        The delay, compared with other countries, in introducing adoption legislation in Britain appears to have been due to a combination of factors. One such factor was the attitude of the propertied classes towards ownership and inheritance and a reluctance that property should be allowed to pass into the hands of 'outsiders' such as adopted children. The first Adoption Act had to compromise on the matter and in England adopted children could not inherit from their parents until 1949 when the law was changed. In Scotland this change had to wait till 1964. A second factor was the social conditions of the 19th century and the prevailing philosophy of 'laisser-faire' which excluded the possibility of special measures being undertaken for the protection, among other things, of deprived children and especially of the illegitimate. The community's concern for the illegitimate child should therefore be seen in relation to the small concern shown towards children from 'ordinary' backgrounds. Attention was first focussed on eradicating the most gross conditions under which children from different walks of life were labouring. This appeared to take some precedence over other considerations, such as the needs of minority groups of which the destitute and illegitimate were only one. The general hostility and moral outrage felt towards the single mother at the time, would not have permitted special measures for her child, before the needs of other children had been met. As modern adoption began to be increasingly associated with illegitimacy, legislation regulating its practice also had to wait for a softening of public attitudes. The third factor was connected with fears about heredity and the transmission of immorality from parent to child. Illegitimate children, it was thought, carried the badness and immorality of their parents. This possibly explains why until the 1940's adoption was mainly confined to the working-classes and it is only since then that adoption as a custom has been fully accepted into the ethos of middle-class society. The number of orphan and illegitimate children resulting from the first Worl War generated a certain amount of sympathy among the upper classes, but there is no evidence to show that any widespread attempt was made to adopt such children. Our findings show that the percentage of middle-class families that adopted through the courts in Scotland in 1935 was only seven per cent, compared to more than five times that percentage in 1965. In 1935 most of the 'middle-class' adopters were small tradesmen but in 1965 they were mostly professional. This cannot be explained entirely by the spread of professionalism in the last thirty years. The main factors that seem to have brought this about are the increased understanding about illegitimacy and knowledge dispelling fears about the hereditary transmission of immorality, combined with importance being placed on environmental influences and emotional attachment. Since the end of the last World War, adoption has become both respectable and fashionable and since the mid-fifties adoptions have been announced regularly in the "Times". The irony of the situation is that now it is much harder for a working-class couple to adopt, because of the criteria used by several agencies in their selection process. The fourth factor, concerns the issue of parental rights and the degree to which these have been held as inalienable. The conflict between the rights of parents and those of children was usually resolved in favour of the first.

The provisions of the 1926 Adoption Act mainly referred to the conditions under which Adoption Orders could be granted, to the jurisdiction of the Courts, to the kind of consent necessary, the appointment of a guardian ad litem and to the effect of adoption orders. The Act also prescribed certain conditions regarding those who could adopt. An adoption order could not be made under the Act except with the consent of a parent or guardian of the infant, but the Act gave power to the Courts to dispense with such consents if certain conditions were satisfied. Such conditions were for parents who could not be found, who had abandoned or deserted the child or who had persistently neglected or refused to contribute to its maintenance. The Act explicitly provided that the Court should be satisfied that the adoption order, if granted, would be for the welfare of the child. Unlike the Guardianship of Infants Act, the Adoption Act of 1926 did not make the welfare of the child "paramount", though it will be argued later on that by implication it did more than the present Adoption Act. The Act also provided for the appointment of a person or a body to act as guardian ad litem to the child, with the main duty of safeguarding the child's interests before the court. There was provision in the Act for de facto adoptions to cover all children who, for the last two years preceding the Act, were in the custody of adoptive parents.

The Registrar-General was directed by the Act to establish and maintain a register to be called the Adopted Children's Register, in which every adoption order would be registered. A certified copy of such an entry would be accepted as evidence of the adoption and a birth certificate could be issued from the Register as if it were "a certified copy of an entry in the Register of Births". The Registrar-General Would also keep an index of the Adopted Children's Register which would be open to public search. Alongside this, he was required to keep a register in such a way that it would be possible to trace the connection between an entry in the Register of Births and its corresponding entry in the Adopted Children's Register. These Registers would not be open to inspection nor would information from them be given except under a Court order. In contrast, in the Scottish Adoption Act of 1930, the provision is made that information from the Register which gives the connection between the entry in the Adopted Children's Register and the original birth entry can be made available to the adopted persons themselves, after they attain the age of seventeen years. Apparently the provision was made to enable adopted children to find out about their biological parents because until 1964 they could inherit only from them and not from their adoptive parents. This provision of the Scottish Act is now hailed as a foresightful piece of social legislation that gave the adopted child the opportunity to find out more about himself and thus strengthen his feelings of identity.

An adopted child can have the equivalent of a birth certificate giving his adopted name, date of birth, and the name, occupation and address of his adopters. No details are given about the biological parents, or the place of birth. In subsequent life situations, such as obtaining a passport or a pension, it is the place of birth which is asked for. It is now possible for an adopted person to obtain a shortened certificate from the Adopted Children's Register which conceals the fact of Adoption and gives no details of parentage. This, we have found, has led to more problems than the ones it was intended to resolve.

The Act of 1926 has formed the basis of present day adoption legislation and subsequent Acts have been noted mainly for their additional provisions and their amendments, designed to reflect some new thinking arising out of experience of applying the Act. From 1926 onwards the number of societies arranging adoptions increased to such an extent that it gave rise to public concern and anxiety. The Act had failed to make provision for regulating the activities of old or new societies and no standards for practice had been laid down. By 1936, adoption societies in England were placing almost one quarter of all children

adopted, without any accountability to the community. In 1936
a Committee under the Chairmanship of Lady Horsburgh, M.P. was
appointed "to enquire into the methods of adoption agencies
and societies and report whether any, and if so what, measures
should be taken in the public interest to supervise or control
their activities".[16]

The Committee, which reported in 1936, gave a number of
examples of hastily and poorly contrived adoptions. Some
children had been placed with blind, deaf or mentally unstable people or with families that wanted to exploit them.
The Committee reported that some of the societies were doing
their selection through correspondence without adequate investigations to satisfy themselves of the suitability of the
applicants. In outlining the duties of adoption societies,
the Committee firmly stated that "the first duty of an adoption society is beyond question to the child". They added
that the child's future was at stake and society, therefore,
should take every reasonable step to satisfy itself as to
the suitability of the prospective adopters on all grounds,
before the child is handed over. Setting the pattern for
some standards in selection, the report stressed that enquiries by societies should go beyond the economic and social
circumstances of applicants, into their suitability on personal grounds. The Committee stressed the need for qualified people to perform this kind of thorough social investigation. Its recommendations resulted in the Adoption of
Children (Regulations) Act, 1939. The Act provided for the
compulsory registration of adoption societies and for regulations to be made about the way they should be run. The
registration of such societies would depend on the competence and fitness of the people employed by them, but the
Act did not specify what it meant by 'competent' and 'fit'.
The regulations also provided that the case of every child,
about to be delivered into the care of adopters, should be
considered by a "case committee" appointed by the society
for this purpose. Also, that every applicant should be
interviewed before placement, by the committee, or its
representative. These regulations have remained almost un-
altered since their inception in 1939. Alterations could
only be made on the basis of relevant information about how
effective the regulations were, but such information was
not forthcoming because of the provision for excessive
secrecy built into the law and because of most societies'
reluctance to evaluate their practices.

Under the 1949 Adoption Act, all adoptions had to be
supervised by the welfare authority for a minimum period
of three months before the order could be granted. The
Act also made provision for the supervision by the local
authority of all the children under nine, placed through
a third party outside their family, and for seven days'
notice to the welfare authority before such a placement.
It placed a ban on British children being adopted by
foreign nationals but this was modified by the 1958

Adoption Act. This latter Act made it possible for a court to grant authority for the transfer of a British child abroad with a view to adoption. A parent's consent could now be dispensed with if it was "unreasonably withheld". The new Act also provided that the child's mother could not give her consent before the child was six weeks old. The 1950 Adoption Act introduced the idea of a serial number allotted by the court to be used on consent forms so that the identity of the adoptive parents would be concealed from the natural parents.

In spite of the legal changes brought about in the post-war years, by 1953 it was again felt that new thinking had to be injected into adoption practice and that the law was for this purpose the best regulator. In January of that year, a Committee was appointed under the Chairmanship of Sir Gerald Hurst "to consider the present law relating to the adoption of children and to report whether any, and if so, what changes in policy or procedure are desirable in the interests of the welfare of children".[17] The Committee reported within a year and the Adoption Act of 1958 incorporated most of the Committee's recommendations. The 1958 Act applies throughout Britain, except for certain modifications to conform to variations of Scottish and Northern Ireland laws and procedures. The new Act gave express power to local authorities to arrange for the adoption of children not necessarily in their care. It extended from seven to 14, the number of days' notice which a third party who arranges an adoption was required to give to the local authority, and it made all third parties respondent to the application. It required that all applicants for an adoption order, other than the father or mother (and his or her spouse) should be required to provide a medical certificate signed by a fully registered medical practioner. The Hurst Committee refused to recommend the prohibition of third party placements, in spite of considerable pressure urging them to do so. The Act introduced a new provision under which a parent's consent could be dispensed with, if the court was satisfied that the parent had persistently failed, without reasonable cause, to discharge the obligations of a parent. Though this section of the Act was heralded as a new provision that would facilitate the adoption of many children whose parents lose interest in them, it will be shown later on that its provisions have hardly been used. It is an interesting example of the difference between identifying a need and knowing how to meet it.

In the summer of 1969 the Home Secretary appointed a departmental Committee to study and review a number of adoption aspects currently regulated by law. The Adoption Act, with its dual purpose of facilitating adoption as a natural child-parent relationship and of strengthening public controls for the protection of the child's interests, assumes a number of things whose validity is still to be proved. Its original failure to make suitable provision for relevant research to be carried out meant that these assumptions could not be tested. Almost all the evidence submitted to the Hurst Committee in 1953 was based on personal views and beliefs. It is gratifying to know that the 1969 Committee has commissioned a few studies that may help it to arrive at some more objective conclusions. The present adoption legislation has no explicit policy behind it and is mainly the result of piecemeal empiricism. It can be argued that we cannot legislate more explicitly on matters about which so little is known. Rightly or wrongly, however, the Act has come to be seen as a regulator of good practice and its minimum requirements have often been interpreted as the desirable level of practice.

CHAPTER   TWO

RESEARCH METHODS AND DESIGN

The Basic Concepts and Objectives.

The chief aim of adoption law in Britain is to facilitate adoption as a natural child-parent relationship and to
safeguard "the welfare of the infant" by satisfying itself
that children are adopted in good adoptive homes where they
will have a chance to develop their full potential. The
process of adoption work may be seen as a continuing series
of assessments, observations and decisions in which a number
of adoption workers, adoption agencies and professionals
from related disciplines take part. Caseworkers are now
predominantly responsible for arranging and supervising adoptions, though ultimate responsibility for the final disposition lies with the court; the latter is bound by the
adoption law to insist upon "a full expert investigation"
before it grants an order and it must be satisfied that
adoption will be for the welfare of the child.

In spite of the serious implications of adoption practice for the lives of many parents and children, there has
been a paucity of studies to identify, describe and evaluate practice. What constitutes adoption policy and practice in Britain is a question that remains, to a large
extent, still unanswered. Though a number of studies in
adoption outcome have been undertaken both here and the
United States, for a number of reasons practice studies
have been lacking. The absence of such studies is a characteristic however, not only of adoption work, but of
social work practice in general. The possible contribution of descriptive and evaluative studies to the development of practice and of the social work profession in
general is only slowly being realised. Doubts and reservations about the value of studies in social work were
originally focussed on evaluative research. The argument has mainly been that such studies were premature.
It also appeared that attempts to assess effectiveness
amounted to casting doubts on the "competence and
integrity" of the social work profession. The attitudes
of adoption workers, and especially of lay committees,
towards research were as much influenced by the wider
reservations of the social work profession as by some
factors peculiar to adoption work as such. The main
obstacles to adoption studies could be summarised as
follows: First, the legal provisions, which prohibited the
disclosure of certain information which resulted in strengthening agency defensiveness and shrouding adoption practice with unnecessary secrecy and mystique. Second, a fear
that research studies, by generalising behaviour, would
minimise the importance of that which is unique to the
individual. Though this is true to a great extent, human

behaviour also follows certain patterns which can have predictive value or point to certain causative trends. Third,
social work practitioners are not only doubtful about the value
and applicability of research findings, but also frustrated by
the research worker's findings relating to the aggregate rather
than to the individual, because this still leaves the practitioner with the responsibility for reaching his own decisions. Fourth, and possibly the most important issue, is that
of confidentiality. Social work traditionally has occupied
itself with the problem of confidentiality in order to safeguard the right to confidentiality of each individual client.
Its importance should not be minimised, especially in the
field of adoption. Social workers, however, are not alone
as a profession in attaching great importance to the need to
safeguard their clients' confidences. Parker,[18] in trying to
dispel such fears remarked that "although research has to
regard individual cases when the data are being collected,
its essential function is to compound and not to individ-
ualise. Consequently results will normally be unaffected by
the restriction that no individual should be identifiable.
Research is usually dealing with sufficiently large numbers
to make such identification impossible".

The basic rationale for our study was that, although
thousands of children are adopted each year in Britain, almost nothing is known of how this is brought about and of
the policies and principles behind it. In spite of almost
forty years experience in adoption work, little effort has
been made to identify its practice and bring together into
a whole the "working rules", hunches, findings, postulates
and concepts acquired in the course of arranging adoptions,
or to generate theoretical formulations about the sociological characteristics of the biological parents, the
children and the adopters. For us the opportunity to do this
came with the amendment to the Act of Sederunt (Adoption
of Children) 1967, making possible the disclosure of information from the courts' files.

Until very recently, adoption studies in the United
States and in Britain have centred mostly on outcome, with
no or little reference to practice, and no study has as
yet attempted to relate outcome to the practices of different agencies. A major limitation of studies in outcome
is that, even when they take some account of agency practices, the findings can only be true in relation to the
placings of a particular agency. Studies in outcome have
also suffered from the lack of vital preliminary information on which to standardise samples, and from a failure
to use each child's "base line" data for measuring improvement rather than assuming that all children start from the
same position. The research workers, with some exceptions,
have relied for their subjects mostly on volunteers, on
school-children or on the clients of psychiatric clinics .
Our present study highlighted some of the deficiences of
a number of studies in outcome which failed to take into

account process and practice.

Specific objectives:

The main purpose of this study was: (i) to obtain an overall view of adoption practice and to identify certain basic data about some of the sociological characteristics of those affected by it; (ii) to identify how adoption agencies and services are administered; (iii) to obtain an accurate description of adoption work as actually practised by the various agencies and parties involved, such as voluntary and statutory agencies and the courts; (iv) to determine the extent of uniformity, agreement and consistency of policy and practice and to identify the decision making process and information on which judgement was based; (v) to evaluate practice in the light of the legal framework, the standards of professional bodies, social work knowledge and research findings from social work and collateral fields such as child development, psychiatry and medicine and (vi) to answer the question how far current practice safeguards 'the welfare of the child'.

Consideration of Method

The objectives of a study determine to some extent the type of methods to be used. The purpose of this study was not to test or demonstrate hypotheses but rather to obtain an accurate description of adoption practices, answer a number of subsidiary questions and evaluate practice against social work theory. The following methods were found to be appropriate for the aims of the study: (a) careful abstracting of data and other relevant information from the case-records of adoption agencies, supervising welfare authorities and the courts, these being supplemented by information obtained from the answers to a postal questionnaire; and (b) the use of appropriate criteria by which to evaluate the emerging practice and the process of decision-making.

(a) The abstraction of data: For an accurate description of practice we decided to rely mostly on the case records of twelve adoption agencies, eight supervising welfare authorities and twenty courts. This is the first time in adoption research in Britain that information from these three types of agencies has been made available for research purposes. The main advantage of such an approach is that what is studied is the actual rather than the assumed practice. The use of case records and of a postal questionnaire were thought to be the least intrusive methods from the agencies' point of view. Though the potential research value of case material has long been recognised, until recently very little use had been made of it. Parker [18] stressed that "the modification of existing policies, the formulation of new ones and the improvement of social work techniques all depend upon the accessibility of past experience". The main disadvantage of case records is that there is no way of knowing to what extent the worker, consciously or

unconsciously, leaves out certain data that might have been
of the utmost importance in the identification and evaluation of practice. The other major difficulty is the fact
that the records are written to fulfil certain agency objectives rather than with any research project in mind. Not all
agencies, for instance, seek out the same basic data, neither
do they see the same things as being important enough to
merit recording. The pilot study we carried out indicated
that one type of agency by itself could not provide the
necessary information which would supply a whole picture of
the adoption situation. This preliminary study pointed to
the need to combine the information contained in the records
of the three different types of agencies. Some basic data,
that we would have liked to include, could not be obtained
except in a patchy way, and eventually had to be dropped. In
this respect, the research worker needs to find a common
denominator, whilst being conscious of the fact that the
value of any findings will be considerably diminished, if he
has to settle for the lowest common denominator.

Descriptive research, of the kind we were pursuing, required the gathering together of certain facts and items
from a series of case records, in some orderly fashion. The
assembling of such items helps to indicate which factors are
constant in the series and how many vary from the average.
Such an assembly also helps to identify the rules or principles on which certain actions are based. A special schedule was devised for abstracting the information from the
case records of the agencies included in the sample. Only
one schedule was used for each separate case but a different colour was used to distinguish between information obtained from the courts, the welfare authorities and the
adoption agencies. Thus a total of 1030 schedules were
originally used, all containing basic information abstrac-
ted from the court records. Of these, 376 schedules representing as many cases were pursued, and supplemented with
information from the records of adoption agencies and welfare authorities. The schedule was devised in such a way
as to permit the combination of information for certain
basic data, and, at the same time, to make possible the
identification of the practices of each individual agency
in each individual case. In this way it was possible to
obtain a picture of the case from the time it started at
the adoption agency, follow it through to the supervising
authority and finally to the court. As there are three
main parties in the adoption situation, i.e. the mother,
the child and the adopters, the schedule was also sub-
divided into three parts, each part being allocated to one
of each of the three parties.

The postal questionnaire was devised in such a way as
to obtain and supplement any information not available from
the sources quoted above. The questionnaire should be seen,
therefore, as a means of eliciting certain aspects of the
"assumed" practice of the agencies and of aiding the

descriptive and evaluative aspects of the study. (The devised schedule and questionnaire appear in the main study.)

(b) Evaluative Methods: The main objective of this part of the study was to evaluate practice and not outcome, including an assessment of information on which vital decisions were made by caseworkers, curators-ad litem and Sheriffs. In our endeavour to appraise the quality rather than the effectiveness of practice, we were faced with the same problems as those faced by research workers studying outcome. We had to decide early on what were the accepted standards of the social work profession in general and in the adoption field in particular, if these were to be used as evaluative criteria. It may be argued that the test of all adoption work lies in how successful the arrangements turn out to be; i.e. if the placement is successful, then the method by which it has been brought about is immaterial. Nevertheless even if studies in outcome were to show that all adopted children were successfully integrated with their adoptive families, we would still need to identify the circumstances under which this was achieved in order to pass it on to new workers and students who would be expected to carry on the practice. We eventually decided to use as evaluative criteria, social work theory and research findings, including the contributions to the adoption field of related studies in medicine, child development and psychiatry. Beyond this, however, it was also decided to use as criteria the requirements of the law as well as the standards recommended by the professional bodies representing the child welfare field. Books, articles from social work and child welfare journals and circulars addressed to adoption agencies, were studied and criteria identified. The profession of social work has made use of a considerable amount of experience from practice and research to build a theory for the profession and to suggest standards for professional practice. We, therefore, felt justified in using the theory and standards of the profession as one of our main criteria in evaluating the quality of practice. Some would query whether social work is a profession at all and the extent to which it has developed and made known theories about its practice that could earn it professional status, or whether the work is still guided by empiricism and personal hunches. Few dispute now the fact that in the last two decades the profession has organised its practice theories and methods and has engaged more in research in order to build up and reinforce its body of knowledge.

A considerable part of this study was taken up by an evaluation of the information on which decisions for the selection of adoptive parents and the granting of adoption orders was based. The selection of adoptive parents, for instance, presents a situation where a caseworker is mainly responsible for making a variety of judgements based on how he "perceives" the applicants. The adoption worker is constantly faced with the difficult task of selecting "good" families that will privide a certain standard of care for

the children who are the responsibility of the agency. This is
done in the knowledge that the qualities of what constitutes a
good or bad parent are rather vague. However, selection reports
prepared by adoption workers for their case committees were
judged on how far they contained the type of information
suggested by social work literature. The curator ad litem's
reports, which formed the main basis of the courts' decisions,
were also judged on how far they reflected the requirements
laid down by the adoption regulations. The need to establish
the basis of the workers' and courts' decisions is bound up
with the recognition that both these people are daily con-
fronted with decision making.

We identified, and grouped under nine topics, the kind of
information suggested by social work literature as a necessary
basis for reaching appropriate decisions in the selection of
adoptive parents. To avoid unnecessary bias and subjectivity
each of the nine topics was further sub-divided into a number
of relevant items In the end, nine topics comprising forty
items were used as criteria and no topic or item was included
over which there was no broad agreement in social work literature. Inspite of considerable care in analysing and
grading the information it cannot be claimed that subjectivity in the assessment was entirely disposed of. All
attempts by one person to assess what another person does
have their difficulties. It is rarely possible to evaluate
comprehensively every aspect of the domain concerned. Some
degree of arbitrariness enters into the rating system. The
direct method usually available in the physical sciences, in
which a number of observations of an attribute (weight,
chemical composition etc.) are made, is not possible in evaluating work in which many intangibles are involved.

The Planning and Sample

Discussions about the feasibility of the study began in
early 1966 when the Secretary of State for Scotland was considering the amendment to the Scottish Act of Sederunt
(Adoption of Children) The purpose of the amendment was to
make it possible for both courts and adoption agencies to
make available to accredited research workers hitherto confidential information about the adoption situation. In the
ensuing months, the writer met representatives of the
Scottish Education Department, courts, adoption societies
and children's departments and discussed in advance plans
for a study in practice. Letters were followed with personal contacts and this resulted in obtaining the co-
operation of all types of agencies with the exception of two
voluntary ones.

The practice of adoption is a very complicated one and
involves a multi-disciplinary approach. There are social,
medico-psychological and legal aspects to be considered.
Because of the complexity of the practice a variety of
disciplines and agencies participate before the child's adoption is finally effected. A descriptive and evaluative study

of the kind we were pursuing had of necessity to include the
practice of all those who play some part in the process. This
holistic approach was further made necessary by the fact that
what one type of agency does, is often affected or determined
by what the previous agency did and what the next one is
about to do. The year chosen for study was 1965, which was
the latest complete year. The main emphasis of this study
is on non-related adoptions as adoptions by relatives are not
usually handled by agencies—such adoptions also present
different characteristics and issues. Three samples were
chosen to be representative of the whole of Scotland:

(i)   A court sample comprising of 20 of the 56 Sheriff
        courts. In 1965 the courts granted a total of
        2014 adoption orders. The twenty courts in the
        sample granted 1525 adoption orders (or 75.6 per
        cent of all orders). Of the 1525 orders, we
        studied a total of 1030, that is 67.5% of the
        orders granted by the surveyed courts or 51.0% of
        all orders granted in Scotland that year.

(ii)   An agency sample comprising twelve adoption agencies
        with 376 cases which were also in the court sample
        under (i). Eight of the 12 agencies were local
        authority ones and the remaining four voluntary.
        (The names of the 12 agencies, which appear later
        in this text, are given in a disguised form.)
        Two voluntary societies, originally approached,
        refused to co-operate and they were replaced. The
        twelve agencies placed between them a total of 376
        children which were among the 1030 studied at the
        courts. The smallest number placed was 8 and the
        biggest 71. The eight local authority departments
        were also carrying out welfare supervision under
        the provisions of the Act and their supervisory
        function was studied in connection with the plac-
        ings of 242 of the 376 children. Thus the cases
        of most of the children were followed through
        from the court sample, to the agency sample (in-
        cluding welfare supervision) and information was
        supplemented, compared or evaluated accordingly.

(iii)   The postal questionnaire: This was sent to the
        46 public and to the eight voluntary societies
        that were operating as adoption agencies in
        Scotland. Replies were received from 42 agencies
        (or 77.8%). Of the 42 agencies, 38 were local
        authority ones and the remaining voluntary. A
        number of agencies replying were unable to supply
        answers to all the questions because of the lack
        of adequate records. Such missing data included
        information on the number of adoptive applicants
        they had in 1965, the number of children accepted
        for placing, the number of 'hard-to-place'
        children placed or awaiting to be placed, the
        number of children they refused to accept and

so on. As the questionnaire was sent out only two years after the end of the year under study, it was surprising to find that some public agencies were unable to provide basic information about children for whom they had accepted responsibility on behalf of the community.

Conclusion:

The orientation of casework towards therapy has resulted in some failure to study and evaluate administrative and casework processes and their effect on practice. We believe that research of this kind can contribute to the development of the social work profession and can be of use to the practitioners.

CHAPTER   THREE

THE GENERAL STATISTICAL BACKGROUND

Courts in Scotland granted only three orders in 1930, the first year the Adoption Act came into power. The number rose to 347 in the following year and reached its highest peak in 1946 when 2292 orders were granted. In 1950 the number dropped to the lowest post-war figure of 1236. Between 1950 and 1959 the numbers fluctuated from around twelve hundred to fifteen hundred. A continued increase in numbers was maintained from the year 1960 onwards. In 1965 the number of orders granted totalled 2018 and in 1969 the figure stood at 2280.

The annual adoption rate per 10,000 children under 18 years of age remained constant at 10.0 for the period 1951 through 1960. From 1961 through to 1969, however, the rate rose to 14.3 per 10,000 children. The increased rate reflected an increase in the number of illegitimate children born during the period, without a corresponding increase in the number of all births. By the end of 1969 there were approximately twenty-eight and-a-half thousand adopted children under eighteen years of age, or approximately 18 for every thousand of the under 18 population. In the United States, the annual adoption rate per 10,000 children under 21 years of age remained constant at 14 to 15 for the period 1951 through to 1961.[19] It is estimated that among the general population of Scotland there are fifty-six thousand adopted people or 1.1% of the population. Kellmer-Pringle estimates that in England and Wales these figures range from 1.3 per cent to 2.0 per cent.[20]

During the five year period from 1936 through 1940 (table 1), the rate of adoption of illegitimate children was 16.2 per cent of all illegitimate children born in that period. The rate rose to 28.5 per cent during the period 1946 through 1950 and between then and the end of 1969 remained constant, ranging from 28.0 to 30.0 per cent. This percentage was maintained irrespective of the number of illegitimate children born each year. In other words, whether the number of illegitimate children born each year increased or decreased, the surrendering rate remained constant ranging from 28 to 30 per cent. This implies that it is the mothers of illegitimate children who, through their surrendering habits, determine the number of children to be adopted each year and that adoptive applicants at the moment have no control over the situation. (Some caution is required in interpreting these figures because we do not know the number of children who are rejected as unadoptable.) Though the mothers' surrendering habits have not changed appreciably over the last twenty years, there are some indications that the rate of surrender may be falling gradually. From 1965 onwards (table 1) the rate fell slowly

from 30.8 to 27.2 in 1968 but this again went up to 30.2 in
1969. The drop between 1965 to 1968 happened in spite of the
fact that the number of illegitimate children born had been
consistently rising. During the eight year period from 1961
to 1969 there was an increase of 44.5% of illegitimate children born, but during the same period the increase in the
number of children adopted increased by almost a similar
percentage to 43.1%. (Though the number of illegitimate
children born in 1969 appears to have dropped, the percentage in relation to total live births was slightly higher
than 1968. This fall was against the background of a drastic fall in all live births.) Perhaps not too much should
be made of the slight drop between 1965 - 1968 but there
are indications that an increasing number of unmarried mothers
who previously tended to surrender their children may be now
choosing to keep them. The explanation for this may be due
either to better social provisions, or to a more tolerant
attitude in the community towards illegitimacy and unmarried parenthood. In fact this drop coincided with a
period when suddenly it was even felt to be fashionable to
give birth to and keep an illegitimate child. Adoption
numbers may further be influenced by the effect of improved
birth control methods and of easier abortion. In the first
nine months of 1969, the number of notified abortions in
Scotland was 2,500. Though a big percentage of these were
to married women, it still remains to be proved whether
there is any similarity in background characteristics between single mothers who abort and those who tend to
surrender their children. Conversely, adoption numbers may
be equally influenced by improved fertility treatment techniques. The quick changes in numbers indicate how the accel-
erating process of social change quickly renders existing
studies of this type out of date. They emphasize the
necessity for more immediate analysis of new ones.

The Relationship between the number of children adopted each year and opportunity to surrender or adopt.

In 1965, the whole of Scotland was served by 54 adoption agencies. This number included both voluntary and
local authority agencies. A relationship between the
number of children adopted each year and the opportunity to
surrender was found by comparing adoptions by non-relatives in the four Scottish cities. (The comparison was made
after standardising the number of illegitimate children
born in each city, the number surrendered and the percentage of the under 18 population.) In the city of Edinburgh,
where there are six adoption agencies, the rate of adoptions was 12.4 per 10,000 children under 18 years of age;
in the city of Glasgow, with only three adoption agencies,
the rate was 6.1; in Dundee with one small local authority department and some coverage from a nearby society,
the rate was 5.4 and in Aberdeen city, where until recently the only adoption agency was the county department,

the rate was only 4 per 10,000 children under 18 years of age.
It thus appears that an increased number of agencies offer
opportunities for the release of a greater percentage of children, and for more adoptive applicants to come forward. Some
of the children adopted in this way might have been left in
long term care and perhaps never been adopted. Adoption work
is a race against time, and having to depend on another
agency to provide the facilities often deters the over-
worked staff of children's departments from acting with the
necessary speed. This may partly explain why in Scotland,
where almost ninety per cent of local authorities operated
as adoption agencies in 1965, 25.0 per cent of illegitimate
children were adopted by non-relatives, compared with 20.0
per cent in England and Wales where only forty per cent of
authorities were acting as adoption agencies.

Table 1. Number of illegitimate children born and number
adopted.@

Period	Illeg. Children born	Illeg. Children Adopted	% of Children Adopted
1936 - 40	5397	873	16.2
1941 - 45	6964	1456	20.9
1946 - 50	5819	1657	28.5
1951 - 55	4259	1290	30.3
1956 - 60	4140	1227	29.6
1961	4648	1418	30.5
1962	5020	1476	29.4
1963	5340	1508	28.2
1964	5628	1723	30.6
1965	5883	1813	30.8
1966	6160	1834	29.7
1967	6663	1917	28.8
1968	6998	1902	27.2
1969	6727	2030	30.2

@ The figures were arranged on five year averages up to and
  including 1960.

Classification of adoptions

Just over ten per cent of children adopted in Scotland
in 1965 (table 2) were legitimate and of these 70 per cent
were adopted by relatives - two thirds by their mothers and
step-fathers. Children born in wedlock formed only three
per cent of those adopted by non-relatives; there was

Table 2. Classification of adopters by the child's legitimacy

(Court sample: N 1030)

	By Non-relatives	Adopted within the family						Total
		Mother & Step-fa.	Both parents	One parent	Grand-parents	Aunts & Uncles	Re-Adopted	
Illegitimate:	752 (73%)	93 (9.0%)	5 (0.5%)	3 (0.3%)	34 (3.3%)	35 (3.4%)	4 (0.4%)	926 (89.9%)
Legitimate:	31 (3%)	50 (4.9%)	—	—	10 (1.0%)	13 (1.2%)	—	104 (10.1%)
TOTAL:	783 (76.0%)	143 (13.9%)	5 (0.5%)	3 (0.3%)	44 (4.3%)	48 (4.6%)	4 (0.4%)	1030 (100%)

only one instance of a legitimate child being adopted by non-relatives whilst the parental marriage was intact. In contrast to these figures, one fourth of the independent non-relative adoptions in the United States in 1960, involved children born in wedlock.

Adoptions by non-relatives amounted to 76 per cent of all adoptions, as compared to approximately 66 per cent in England and Wales and 53 per cent in the United States. Five children in the sample (or 0.5%) were adopted by their mother and father because at the time of birth the parents were not free to marry. Only three children (or 0.3%) were adopted by their mothers alone and two children were both adopted by their alleged father. Four children (or 0.4%) were re-adopted by their adoptive mothers and their husband, following the death of the adoptive father. Fifteen of the 23 legitimate children who were adopted by relatives were the children of widowed, divorced or separated, parents.

Fifty-two of the children (or 5.0%) were formerly in the care of a local authority and two thirds of these were adopted by their foster-parents. (We did not include among this number babies who were deemed to be 'in care' for a few days or weeks. This step was taken by local authorities to ensure payment of fostering fees and of other expenses in case the mothers were unable to meet these commitments. For purposes of this study, these were not considered as 'in care' cases.)

CHAPTER FOUR

THE NATURAL PARENTS

Illegitimate children form 97 per cent of all children adopted by non-relatives. When we talk, therefore, of the parents of adopted children, we generally refer to single, unwed girls and occasionally to married women who conceive extra-maritally. Just under a third of all illegitimate children born in Scotland each year are adopted, a quarter of them outside their families.

Authoritative studies about the characteristics of mothers giving birth to illegitimate children are rare and at the same time either out of date or carried out in countries or areas with different socio-cultural influences. In an attempt to pre-dict the disposition decision of mothers a few studies have recently appeared comparing the background characteristics and circumstances of single mothers who surrender with those who keep their children. Because of the limitations of the data and the absence of accurate measuring standards, such studies have mainly concentrated on identifying and comparing tangible characteristics, and aspects of personality and relationships have not been fully explored. The studies are agreed about the influence of certain factors on the adoption decision but they also show considerable differences and contradictions which may reflect socio-cultural differences. Adoption case-workers, who frequently have to support mothers through periods of indecision and fluctuation, have often felt that adoption practice could be considerably improved, if more was known about the background characteristics of single mothers, the timing of their decision to keep or surrender and the factors that appear to influence such a decision. Administratively it could help agencies to arrange place-ments with greater certainty, and also to plan for appropriate resources for those mothers who do not surrender immediately after birth or who do not surrender at all.

The Timing of the Mother's Decision

However difficult the mother's situation may be, sooner or later she must make a decision about the baby. Her anxiety, and that of those around her, is usually increased because of certain inherent conflicting needs aroused by the situation. One such conflict, for instance, is the need to place the child as early as possible whilst at the same time giving the mother time to make up her mind in an unhurried way. Other requirements, such as insistence that every mother should be made to see her baby after birth, or that all mothers must breast-feed their children whilst in a Mother and Baby Home, or again that every mother must agree to her child being fostered first before it is finally placed for adoption, add to the existing anxieties and conflicts. Such blanket requirements also fail to take into account in-dividual circumstances and wishes. Equally rigid is the practice followed by a minority of agencies who have elevated the 'giving of psychological insight' to unmarried mothers, as their primary goal. Apart from the inappropriateness of the notion of 'giving', the methods used to achieve such an objective, usually fail to take into account each mother's readiness and capacity to benefit from them, and often fail to attend to other important needs.

As our study consisted of mothers whose children were eventually adopted, the characteristics of these mothers could not be compared with those who kept them. Some of their characteristics, however, were compared with national figures referring to all illegitimate births. A retrospective study of the 368 mothers in the sample showed that two-thirds of them (table 3) made a final decision to surrender either before or within a week after confinement, whilst the rest did so at various intervals later.

Table 3. The Timing of the Mother's Decision

(Agency sample N.368[@])

		Child Adopted	
		N	%
(i)	Decision reached before confinement and constant thereafter	227	61.7
(ii)	Decision reached within a week following confinement and constant thereafter	18	4.9
(iii)	Decision reached when child was over a week old	121	32.9
(iv)	Mixed feelings up to the court stage	2	0.5
	TOTAL	368	100

[@] The original sample was 376 but eight of the children were legitimate and therefore excluded.

These findings suggest a slightly lower percentage of mothers who reached a decision within a week after confinement compared with the findings of studies by Meyer, Jones and Borgatta,[21] Yelloly,[22] and Triseliotis,[23] which showed that almost four out of every five mothers reached a decision within a week after confinement. The explanation of the difference appears to be due mainly to the presence, in this study, of a number of foster-children whose mothers made up their minds at various periods within a span of three years following the child's birth. This loaded the sample with a number of backlog cases that would not have appeared in an ordinary sample.

Forty-nine of the mothers (or 13.3%) appeared to go through a very distressing period during the first few weeks after surrender, but in spite of this they kept to their original decision. All these mothers wrote one or more letters to the respective agency asking for news about the baby and for photographs to be sent to them or suggested sending gifts to the child. Some of the letters were per-meated with considerable guilt and remorse and in all of them there was a tone of sadness and anguish. Through the letters the mothers appeared to **be** trying to retain some link with the baby and their reaction was reminiscent of the reactions of bereaved people. Whilst finding it hard to accept the loss they sustained, they were at the same time mourning for the loss. Even some of the mothers who had received some kind of casework help appeared to need to reflect again on their decision. A further sixteen mothers, however, (or 4.4%) answered agency letters in a very matter of fact way, betraying no emotion and making no requests for further in-formation. The letters had a business-like tone about them and most of the mothers said in them that they wanted to finish with the matter once and for all and not to have to reflect back on it. The extent to which they were suppress-ing or denying their feelings, because they could not face the pain involved, could not be ascertained. We have been told by both hospital and agency workers, that some of the mothers are so distressed about the surrender that they are reluctant to come back to the agency where the relinquish-ment took place. Both places appear to be associated with pain and loss in the minds of the mothers and are therefore to be avoided as far as possible. For this type of mother, any casework help can only be offered before or during con-finement, otherwise she is likely to become inaccessible.

Factors Affecting the Timing of the Mothers' Adoption Decision

Of seven identifiable factors i.e. age, occupation, social class, education, movement before confinement, home background and parity, two factors appeared to be closely associated with the timing of the decision. These were movement before confinement and social class. Two other factors which suggested themselves were education and occu-pation but because of the absence of comparative figures these could not be verified. Of the 245 mothers who moved before confinement to another area to avoid embarrassment, 85.0 per cent reached their decision to surrender before or

within a week after confinement. In contrast, of 123 mothers
who did not move, only just under half reached a similar
decision within the same period. Similarly, of 164 mothers
employed in professional, technical or secretarial occupations or studying or training for these occupations, 84.0 per
cent moved to a new area before their confinement and nine
out of ten reached their decision to surrender before or
within a week after confinement. In contrast, of 182 mothers
occupied in the distributive trades, in skilled manual jobs,
in transport, catering, domestic jobs and in factories, only
just over half moved to another area before confinement. Of
those who moved, three out of every four reached their decision to surrender before or within a week after confinement.
In conclusion well over four out of every five mothers, who
move before confinement and eventually surrender, are likely
to reach their decision before or within a week after confinement and this possibility is greatly increased if the
mother is also employed in, or studying or training for one
of the professions.

Background Characteristics of the Biological Parents.

Meyer, Jones and Borgatta,[21] who compared the characteristics of mothers who surrendered with those who kept their
children, found that the following factors had a positive influence on the adoption decision of white girls: non-
catholic religion, college education, aged under 18 and the
putative father being a single man. Yelloly's [22] study
showed that the decision to surrender was related to the
presence of other children of the natural mother, the putative
father being a married man and the mother's parents attitude
being negative. Gill [24] claims that of three factors, social
class, age and parity, the adoption decision-making process
was influenced only by social class.   Triseliotis [25] found
that the characteristics associated with the decision of
single girls to surrender were: negative family attitude,
social class I and II, movement away from usual address before confinement and the putative father being a married
man. It is noted that the various studies quoted are agreed
only on some characteristics as influencing the adoption-
making process. A possible explanation is that the differences may reflect specific cultural attitudes and social
factors characteristic of the areas where the studies took
place.

(i) Parental Age

(a) Age of Natural Mothers: Over a third of the mothers who
surrendered (table 4) were under twenty years old at the
time of the child's birth; almost two-fifths were between
twenty and twenty-four and just over a quarter were twenty-
five and over.

Our sample of adopted children shows a higher percentage of mothers under 25 surrendering their babies compared

with the same age-group of all mothers giving birth to an illegitimate child. This, however, can create a false picture of
the actual situation. The high percentage of mothers under 25
surrendering is explained by the fact that only a small number
of "ever married" women appear in the adoption sample, compared with their estimated number among all mothers giving
birth to an illegitimate child. The Registrar General's figures, include all mothers giving birth to an illegitimate child
irrespective of status and include at least one third who are
married, separated, divorced or widowed and who are generally
older than single mothers. No evidence was found to support
the view that young mothers, especially those under 18, would
mostly surrender their children because of the lack of the
physical and emotional resources to support them.

Table 4. Age of Mothers Surrendering (Agency Sample N.368)

Mother's Age	Child Adopted		All mothers giving birth to an illeg.child in 1965[@]
	N	%	%
Under 20	129	(35.1)	27
20 - 24	140	(38.0)	32
25 - 29	57	(15.5)	20
30 and over	42	(11.4)	21
TOTAL	368	(100)	100

[@] Report of the Registrar-General for Scotland-1965.

(b) Age of Putative Fathers: Information on this group of
fathers is always very difficult to obtain but as five of the
12 agencies in the sample included such information, it was
decided to include it. One in every six fathers was under
twenty at the time of the child's birth; two in every five
were between 20 and 24, almost a quarter were between 25
and 29 and the remaining one fifth were thirty and over.
Not unexpectedly, putative fathers were generally older than
the mothers. However, in spite of the apparent differences,
only in seven per cent of the cases was the father older by
more than five years than the mother. This was a lower
percentage compared with that found between adoptive mothers
and fathers. On the basis of this, it would be difficult to
describe putative fathers as "fatherly" figures to young
teenagers.

(ii) The Marital Status of the Natural Parents

(a) The marital status of the mothers: Though illegitimate births do not occur to single mothers only, official statistics do not distinguish between the unmarried and "ever married" women. Independent studies in different parts of Scotland suggest, however, that approximately one third of illegitimate pregnancies each year occur to "ever married" or co-habiting women. In the last ten years there has been a slight decline in the number of illegitimate maternities to women "ever married" or co-habiting and this may be related to increased resort to, or avialability of divorce.

Of the 368 children adopted by non-relatives, only 45 (or 12.2%) were born to "ever married" women. If the various studies suggest that approximately one third of all illegitimate pregnancies occur to "ever married" women, then their percentage representation in the adoption group suggests that the rate of surrender by them is well below that of single mothers. The suggestion is that when the mother of an illegitimate child is married, separated, divorced or widowed, it is more likely that the child will be kept than surrendered.

(b) The marital status of putative fathers: Just over four fifths of the fathers whose illegitimate children were adopted in 1965 were single men and the remaining 17.1% were either married or separated but not free to marry. Consideration of the marital status of the father was suggested by the theory that when a girl has relationships with a man who is not free for marriage she will, upon becoming pregnant, perpetuate her deviance for the same psychological reasons that led to her situation by tending to keep rather than surrender the baby. Yet Yelloly and Triseliotis both found that the decision of single mothers to surrender was positively influenced in cases where the putative father was a married man.

(iii) The Parents' Socio-economic Background

(a) Social Class: (table 5) shows a very high rate of surrender among mothers classified in the two upper groups and a considerably lower rate among girls from semi-skilled, and even lower from unskilled occupations. Though only about eleven per cent of all illegitimate children were born to mothers in social class I and II, such children formed almost a fifth of all adoptions. In contrast, though almost half the number of illegitimate children were born to mothers of semi-skilled and unskilled occupations, such children formed only 28.6% of those adopted.

The absence of reliable statistics, on a national level, makes it difficult to establish the relationship between illegitimacy and social class. A study of the figures published by the Registrar-General for Scotland from 1950 onwards shows that in the earliest years, the highest ratio of illegitimate children occurred in social class IV, then V, then III and II and only an insignificant ratio in social class I. By 1968

the picture had changed, showing a considerable rise in the
ratio of social class I, II and III. At the same time there
was no fall in the ratio of social class IV and V. The highest ratio in 1968 was in social class IV, then II, then III,
then V and I. The rise in social class I and II may partly
represent an increase of female occupations in this class
or it may be that illegitimacy is gradually spreading among
the more sophisticated classes in spite of greater aware-
ness of contraceptive facilities among this group of women.
It is also of interest to note the high rate of surrenders
among this latter group compared to mothers from the two
lower classes.

Table 5. _The social class background of mothers
surrendering (Agency sample N.368)

Social Class	Child Adopted		All illeg. births[@]
	N	%	%
I and II (Mainly profess- ional)	65	(18.8)	10.8
III – Skilled	182	(52.6)	41.3
IV and V – Semi skilled and unskilled	99	(28.6)	47.9
	346	(100)	100
School-girls and housewives	22		
TOTAL	368		

(b) Occupation: The biggest occupational group of mothers surrendering their children was that of clerical and secretarial
workers (table 6) followed by mothers employed in the professions.

   The most common occupations of mothers of professional
and semi-professional background were nursing, teaching and
studying or training for the professions. These were the ones
that appeared to experience the greatest pressure from their
families to surrender. Some of the pressure, however, came
also from themselves and a considerable number said that the
main reason for surrendering the baby was to be free to get
on with their studies or with their professions. The reason
why few girls of unskilled occupations surrender their

children may reflect social and cultural attitudes towards illegitimacy. Such evidence comes mainly from sources dating from the last century and characteristic attitudes are elaborated upon in the writings of Crammond.[3]

Table 6. The occupations of mothers (Agency sample N.368)

		N	%
(i)	Professional, technical, managerial (includes students)	65	(18.8)
(ii)	Clerical and secretarial	99	(28.6)
(iii)	Distributive workers	19	(5.5)
(iv)	Skilled manual	64	(18.5)
(v)	Transport, catering, laundry etc.	64	(18.5)
(vi)	Domestic	21	(6.1)
(vii)	Factories, mills, labourers, warehouses	14	(4.0)
		346	(100)
	Schoolgirls and housewives	22	
	TOTAL	368	

The Occupational Background of Putative Fathers: Almost a third of the fathers were in the professional, technical and managerial group, one in every ten were in clerical jobs, two out of every five in skilled occupations and the remaining one fifth were in semi-skilled and unskilled occupations. (This group included 21 students.)

(iv) Educational Background of Natural Mothers

Almost two-thirds of the mothers, whose children were adopted in 1965, had left school at the age of fifteen. A further 13 per cent had stayed beyond the statutory school-leaving age, 18.0 per cent had attended or were still attending college or university and 3.3% were still at school. One girl in every fifteen became pregnant within a year after leaving school at fifteen. Meyer, Jones and Borgatta,[21] as well as Triseliotis,[23] claim from their studies that there is a close association between the decision to surrender and education beyond compulsory school-age. In fact, this last factor seems to be more closely associated with the decision to surrender than social class, but comparative statistics are rather inadequate.

(v) <u>Movement Away From Usual Address Before Confinement</u>

One of the main repetitive characteristics the study came across was the considerable number of mothers who had changed their home-address for another area when their confinement was drawing near. Of the 368 mothers in the adoption sample, 214 (or 58.2 per cent) had moved from their usual address to a city or town other than their own and a further 31 (or 8.4 per cent) had moved to another address within the same city – usually a Mother and Baby Home. Only under a third of the mothers did not move. (When analysing these figures, care was taken not to include mothers who moved from their usual address simply because of the absence of maternity facilities in the area where they usually lived.) When these figures are compared with those for mothers who kept their babies and subsequently adopted them, alone or jointly with their husbands, the vast majority of mothers who kept their babies did not move from their usual address. Of 93 such mothers only nine had moved from their usual address to another area. These findings appear to support the view that change of address before confinement is strongly associated with the decision to surrender. Mothers in our sample moved to another area mostly to avoid embarrassment to themselves and to their families. A further analysis of the figures, by occupation, showed that the highest percentage of those who moved were in the professional, technical, managerial and clerical group and almost 85 per cent of these released their children.

(vi) <u>Incomplete Family Background</u>

Since the publication of studies on emotional deprivation, considerable attention has been focussed on the background experiences of people who have been identified as 'social deviants' or as psychologically disturbed. A number of studies suggest that a certain amount of delinquency, mental illness and other forms of emotional disturbance are related to early childhood experiences of deprivation arising from the emotional or physical loss of one or both parents without subsequent compensating and satisfying experiences. Thirty-two per cent of the mothers in our sample had lost one or both parents through death, separation or divorce, before they reached the age of sixteen. Another five per cent came from homes where there was chronic illness and disability. A significant point about the mothers who lost one or both parents was that two-thirds of them had lost a father and only one third had lost a mother or both a mother and a father. Though it still has to be established that the broken home is more characteristic of unmarried mothers than of other women in the community, the importance of the father's absence to the growing adolescent girl merits further study. Vincent [25] et al in his comprehensive study of unmarried mothers revealed that a control group of single-never-pregnant girls, with socio-economic backgrounds similar to the unwed mothers he studied, had an almost idential rate of

broken homes in their childhood (35.4 per cent for the unwed
mothers versus 31.1 per cent for the single-never-pregnant
girls).

(vii) Multiparous Mothers

Just over 10.0% of the children adopted in 1965, were
born to multiparous women. Whether the mother kept or surrendered her first baby, this had no important influence on
the decision about the second or subsequent child. In contrast to the general sample, multiparous women who surrendered were mostly of semi - skilled and unskilled occupations.

(viii) Religious Background

Though the study pointed to a significant relationship
between a Roman Catholic background and the mother's tendency
to keep her child, further studies are needed in connection
with this characteristic because of the way Catholic mothers
are concentrated in certain areas. Some Catholic workers
would encourage surrender only in exceptional cases, whilst
others would go along with the mother's decision. A separation of mother and child does not appear to be easily accepted in areas with strong Catholic influence.

(ix) The Duration of the Parents' Relationship

Writing about the motivation for an out-of-wedlock pregnancy, Young [26] comments that "a considerable percentage of
the mothers either do not know the man at all, or have had
only a brief, casual relationship with him. Frequently they
do not even know his name". Young, by implication, associates neurotic personality with short and casual relationships
entered into by the "parents". Relationships between human
beings are of an infinite variety and their measurement is not
easy. The information contained in the records of five of the
12 agencies gave only the simple indication of the duration of
the relationship between the mother and the alleged father,
with no indication of the quality of the feeling involved. No
more than a quarter of the relationships could be described as
casual, having lasted less than six months. Over a fifth
lasted from 6 to 12 months and the remaining for over a year,
(31.0% lasting for two years or more). On the basis of these
findings, it would be difficult to conclude that the parents'
relationships were brief or casual, recognising at the same
time that even short relationships can have a considerable
amount of emotional investment.

(x) Personality Characteristics

An out-of-wedlock pregnancy presents problems in terms of
the immediate necessity for adequate medical care, very often
for special accommodation to be provided, for the need to
maintain secrecy, for adequate financial support and above all
for a decision to be made about the child's future. It is
generally agreed that the experience of pregnancy creates a
state of normative crisis not only for the single expectant
woman but for the married woman as well. With the additional

pressures to which the unmarried pregnant woman is exposed, it is not surprising to find an intensification of the reactions common in her married counterpart, with many mixed feelings about the future of the baby. During the past twenty years or so a number of empirical and descriptive studies tried to throw some light on the complex combination of motives and circumstances that lead to unmarried parenthood. Some studies have stressed the cultural and social factors, such as the presence or absence of social stigma, and the extent to which socially inculcated guilt surrounds illegitimacy. Others have stressed group pressures and the need for experimentation, especially at the vulnerable stage of adolescence. The one exposition that appears to have gained most ground is the psychoanalytic one which claims that unmarried parenthood is rarely accidental and that the pregnancy represents the single woman's solution of her intra and inter-personal problems. In all these women, it is claimed, there is a strong unconscious desire to become pregnant.

Because of the very scanty and factual nature of the records studied, it was not possible to identify any particular personality traits or characteristics associated with the adoption decision. Yelloly [22] noted from her study that the percentage of "unstable" mothers who kept their children was higher than the percentage of such mothers who surrendered them. Vincent [27] also concluded that a constellation of personality characteristics, found with unmarried mothers who keep their baby, imply general immaturity. In contrast, Wright [28] and Levy [29] claim that a majority of the women who kept their children made a remarkably good life for themselves and their children. Even the so-called border-line cases were able to manage fairly well in comparison with the total population. There is urgent need for research in this area to examine personality and attitudinal variables, holding constant the social background characteristics which are found to be predictive of the mother's decision.

Our general observations from the limited information at our disposal indicated the great diversity of the personalities and of the social and sub-cultural backgrounds of the single mothers, with an age-range stretching from the schoolgirl of thirteen or fourteen to the middle-aged woman. All types of girls, with different personalities, diverse social backgrounds and with different strengths and needs appeared to get pregnant. Many had experienced physical and emotional deprivation and the baby appeared to represent an attempt to deal with their problems and conflicts. For others, the pregnancy itself created problems of relationship. Their reactions varied enormously, depending on the girl's personality. Some were shattered by the experience and felt that they could never carry through; others adopted a blase attitude towards their pregnancy, denying all their feelings of guilt and fear and insisting that they could cope on their own and that they were not worried about the situation. And there were those who reacted in a realistic and mature way making adequate plans for themselves and the children.

(xi) Reasons for Surrendering the Child

Of 118 mothers who surrendered their child and whose explanation for this was included in curators' reports, almost half implied that they did this because they could not support it; a quarter explained that they wanted to give the child an opportunity to grow up with both a father and a mother and the remaining quarter stated that they wanted to carry on with their studies, training or occupations. More of the mothers studying or holding professional or secretarial occupations said that they wanted to be free to get on with their studies or jobs, whilst a majority of girls employed in semi-skilled and unskilled occupations implied that the main reason was the lack of adequate and financial family support. The more altruistic explanation of giving the child the opportunity to be brought up by a father and mother was made by girls from every kind of background.

III

Parents Adopting Their Own Children

The motives behind adoptions by natural parents are very obscure, especially as it is a practice followed by a minority of parents. It does appear, however, that the motives behind a fair number of such adoptions cannot be entirely divorced from the circumstances that bring about the marriage itself. It is possible for a parent to apply to adopt his own child alone, or if married, jointly with his/her spouse and 15% of orders granted in Scotland in 1965 came under this category. Of the 155 such adoptions, in our court sample, 143 were orders granted to mothers adopting jointly with their husbands. Of the 143 such adoptions, 50 orders were on behalf of legitimate children who were adopted by their mother and her second husband; in 85.0% of these cases the previous marriage was dissolved.

Adoptions by parents are not subject to welfare supervision. The only person that ever gets in touch with the family is the curator ad litem. Curators see these as routine petitions and the petitioners too saw the granting of the orders as a formality. No reservations were expressed on any of these adoptions by either the curator or the Sheriff. In five cases in which the children in question were five years or older, the parents had not yet explained to them their true relationship within the family. Curators generally accepted the parents assurance that they would tell the children when older. The Courts too accepted this statement. The need of children to know the truth about their parentage appeared to have been underestimated. (Preliminary findings from a study currently being carried out by the writer into the feelings and views of adopted adults, reveal that their main distress is their adopted parents' refusal to tell them about their adoption and their reluctance to talk about it.) The objectives met by granting orders to mothers and their husbands are rather unclear, though slightly different issues are raised in the case of the adoption of legitimate children following their mothers' remarriage from those of the illegitimate child.

(i) The adoption of legitimate children by a parent: The advantages of an adoption order for the legitimate child appear to be as follows: (a) a formal liability for maintenance will be laid on the step-father: (b) in the case of the father dying intestate, the child is not debarred from sharing in the inheritance: (c) the child can bear the surname of the household in which he lives: (d) it is a safe-guard against possible interference by the biological father; and (e) it can add to a sense of security and belonging. With the exception of (a) and (e) all the other three advantages can be conferred on the child administratively, provided that the step-father is motivated enough to draw up his will, the child changes his name by deed of poll and in the case of interference by the natural father the court machinery is used. Liability for maintenance by a step-father is likely to arise only in very rare circumstances. The final advantage appears to be the more important but also the more elusive. Some would argue that, if the personal relationship is strong and the child is accepted for what it is, then the making of the order is immaterial. Many step-fathers who are equally interested in their step-children refrain from adopting them. There was no case in our sample of a step-mother applying jointly to adopt her husband's child.

The disadvantages for the legitimate child may be summed up as being: (a) a shortened birth-certificate with all its connotations; (b) a change of surname and or Christian name that may have repercussions on the child's sense of identity; (c) the child may be used to cement an insecure marriage; and (d) if adoption takes place when the child is very young there is a real risk that the truth about his parentage may not be disclosed to him. On balance it is very doubtful whether there is any real advantage to the child in allowing such adoptions, whilst the adoption situation introduces a number of complications connected with personal relationships. A form of guardianship arrangement could secure similar benefits to the child without the emotional implications of the adoption situation.

None of the fathers of the legitimate children refused to give their consent and with the exception of three, the remainder had either disappeared or were not at the time interested in what happened to the child. Two fifths of the children were between six and nine years old at the time of their adoption, another third were over ten and the remaining 16 were under six. Only two of the children aged above ten were consulted by the curator ad litem about

their impending adoption. Almost a fourth of the 'parents'
applied for an order within three months following their
marriage. The speed with which these couples acted could be
connected with a desire to make the child feel as one of the
family before a child of the marriage was born.

(ii) <u>The adoption of illegitimate children by their mothers
and step-fathers</u>: Some of the arguments advanced for and
against the adoption of legitimate children by their mothers
and step-fathers, apply also to the adoption of illegitimate
ones. The motivation for these adoptions is again very unclear.
Only a fraction of the mothers who marry someone who is not
the father of the child, proceed to adopt jointly. It is difficult to say whether it is the more insecure ones who proceed
to do so or, on the contrary, it is those with more forethought
and greater understanding of their children's needs.

A closer study of the 93 children (52 male and 41 female)
showed that four out of every five were less than six years
old at their mother's marriage. Well over half of the
petitions in this category were submitted within 12 months of
the date of the marriage. The speed of the action suggested
a wish to finalise the adoption before children of the
marriage were born. It could also imply a wish to blot out
the past both for the parent and for the child. The desire
of the mother to provide a father-figure, especially to a
male child, possibly motivated a number of marriages and subsequent adoptions. Considerable anxieties about discipline
and control are usually raised for the single parent, and
these may be greater in the case of male children. (More male
children were adopted in this category than female. In view
of the fact that more illegitimate male children are also
adopted by non-relatives, the question that arises is what
happens to the girls. One possible explanation is that girls
do not raise similar anxieties in their mothers as do boys.
Child guidance experience indicates that the age between two
and five usually faces the single parent of a male child with
considerable problems of control. Recourse to marriage may
be one of the solutions suggesting themselves, along with
the popular view that a boy needs a father-figure.) This explanation could suggest that it is the more insecure mothers
who tend to follow this practice; at the same time, however,
we found that of the 93 children who were adopted in this
way, all but seven were continuously in the care of their
mothers since birth, two had been in the care of local authorities and the remaining five were looked after by grand-
parents. These figures would suggest that it is the more
'stable' mothers who appear to apply to adopt jointly with
their husbands, unless unmarried mothers who keep their
children manage better than is generally assumed.

As a group, the mothers in this category, were older at
marriage (24.8 years) than the general population, (23.4 years)
but younger compared to non-related adoptive mothers (25.2
years). The average age of their husbands at marriage was
29.3 years. One mother in five married a man at least ten

years older than herself, but equally one in five married a man younger than herself by one to five years.

Summary Characteristics

Four common characteristics could be identified for both the group of mothers who surrendered and for those who kept their illegitimate children and subsequently adopted them jointly with their husbands. These were age, social class, occupation and movement. The age-range of mothers who kept and of those who surrendered had close similarities, but otherwise the mothers who surrendered were mostly from a social class background I, II and III, were occupied in professional or clerical jobs and had moved to another area for a considerable period before confinement. In contrast, the mothers who kept their children and later adopted them, were mostly from social class background V, IV and III, were working in factories, mills, breweries and warehouses as unskilled, semi-skilled and skilled workers, and only a few had moved away from their usual residence well before confinement to avoid embarrassment to themselves and their families. The association between the adoption decision and the three characteristics: social class, occupation and movement before confinement, was statistically significant at the 5% significance level. Social class and occupation are obviously closely related and we might ask whether both of these characteristics do provide additional information with which to predict the adoption decision.
This had been investigated and it was found that occupation provides additional information than social class. The latter characteristic can therefore be excluded from the list of three quoted earlier.

CHAPTER   FIVE

THE FUNCTION, MANAGEMENT AND RESOURCES
OF ADOPTION AGENCIES

The Function of Adoption Agencies

Adoption agencies are non-profit making, voluntary or
public agencies whose primary purpose is social service, subject to legal and community control. Their general aim is to
bring together applicants eager to adopt and parents who are
anxious for some reason or other to surrender their children.
There is no bar to adoptions being arranged by any individual
acting as 'third party' or by the parent of the child acting
independently.

The representatives of the 12 agencies in our "agency
sample" were broadly agreed about the function of their
agencies and the kind of services they set out to provide. All
believed that they were offering appropriate services to:-

    (i)   Unmarried mothers who surrender their children
            for adoption;

    (ii)   Children surrendered for adoption; and

    (iii)   Adoptive parents during the selection and post-
            placement supervisory period.

How Adoptions were Arranged in 1965

In the last twenty or so years considerable anxieties
have been expressed about the supposedly large number of adoptions being arranged by 'third parties'. Witnesses,
giving evidence to the Hurst committee, [17] stressed that
'third party' adoptions and direct placements by parents were
undesirable and "wholly unsuitable". It was estimated that
approximately one third of adoptions each year were arranged
by a third party. Most writers lumped together 'third party'
and direct placements by parents, failing to identify the
different characteristics that distinguish the two groups
from each other. Table 7 shows that, contrary to earlier
assumptions, only a very small proportion, under five per
cent, of children were placed with non-relatives either by
a 'third party' or directly by a parent. In six of the 24
direct placements, the children were placed with neighbours
or friends following the death of the mother. The friend
taking over the child had cared for it during the mother's
illness. A major drawback of direct placements generally
is the possibility of continued contact between natural
parents and adoptive parents which carries risks of
interference and increased confusion for the child.

The small number of 'third party' and direct placements found in this study appear to be connected with: (i)
the comparative availability and accessibility of adoption

agencies throughout Scotland; ninety per cent of local authorities in Scotland (compared to only 40% in England) were
operating as adoption agencies; (ii) the flexibility shown by
many agencies in such matters as selection, timing of the
placements, non-insistence on a pre-adoption placement, age
qualifications and so on.

Table 7. Adoptions by Non-relatives and the way
          they were arranged   (Court Sample N.783)

		N	%
(i)	Arranged by vol. adoption societies	400	(51.1)
(ii)	Arranged by children's departments	347	(44.3)
(iii)	Arranged by a third party	12	(1.5)
(iv)	Arranged by a parent directly	24	(3.1)
		783	(100)

     Ten of the twelve third party adoptions were arranged by
professional people such as vicars, solicitors, hospital matrons,
doctors and so on. They placed the children mainly with adopters from a similar socio-economic background to that of themselves and of the mothers. (In contrast direct-placements were
mostly arranged by parents of a lower socio-ecomonic background
placing the children with couples of a similar background to
themselves.) The attraction of third party adoptions appear to
be connected with the satisfaction of caring for a baby almost
from birth and perhaps with certain applicants, dislike of the
scrutiny and investigations involved in agency selections.
The process can also be quicker and the possibility of rejection does not arise. Contrary to fears expressed in the
House of Commons recently, no evidence was found to suggest
any "illicit traffic" in babies.

     Third party adoptions are generally frowned upon by rec-
ognised agencies because of: (a) the total absence of casework services to the parties involved and especially to the
mother; (b) the haste with which some of these are arranged;
(c) being local, and lacking the protection from the privacy
of secrecy and distance. (This was not true of the cases in
our sample); (d) greater health-hazards for the adopters;
and (e) being arranged mainly with the interests of the
adopters in mind and without sufficient investigation into
the suitability of the applicants. The Hurst committee [17]
resisted considerable pressure to recommend the prohibition
of third party and direct placements, because of the absence
of conclusive evidence about their adverse effects. The
small number of third party placements found in this study

does not appear to justify any such drastic action, especially as it will be shown later, that a fair number of agency place-ments are not generally arranged with more care. It is still possible within the present system to allow for choice, with-out it necessarily being to the detriment of the child. Direct placements may have to be regulated differently.

The Management and Resources of Voluntary Adoption Societies

In 1965 Scotland was served by eight voluntary adoption societies. Five of these were based in Edinburgh, two in Glasgow and one in Perth. The societies were run by committees which appeared to be responsible for three levels of decision-making:

(i)   Administrative and financial decisions which determined the size and scope and the range of services to be offered;

(ii)   professional policy decisions which determined general eligibility and other criteria for accepting children and adopters;   and

(iii)   individual case decisions.

Except for one society where these three levels of decision-making could be clearly distinguished, the function of the committees of the rest of the societies was difficult to identify. In some instances the same committee or the same individuals carried on a variety of functions transcending the three aspects described above. In the case of the non-denominational societies accountability appeared to rest in the annual general meeting, but with sectarian ones this was unclear.

A study of the membership of the various committees con-firmed the established image of voluntary societies as middle-class institutions managed and controlled by people from a similar background. In some of their decision-making they tended to give expression to attitudes and values commonly held by this section of the community.

The Adoption Agency Regulations of 1959 require each society to appoint a separate 'case committee' whose main responsibility will be to approve the child's placement. The function of case committees, as set out in the Regu-lations, is open to several interpretations. As the Regulations now stand, a case committee may choose to make decisions by relying on reports from its staff, or conduct interviews or pay home visits to assess applicants, thus by-passing its professional staff. The study showed that case committees varied in their practices and much depended on individual interpretations. The lack of clear boundaries between their function and that of the professionals has perhaps contributed to the perpetuation of a rather ama-teurish approach by some societies towards their adoption

work.   Though adoption work involves decisions with an emphasis
on the social component, only one of the societies had a trained
social worker as a co-opted member on one of its committees.
In contrast, all societies had doctors, ministers of religion,
solicitors, health visitors etc., on their committees, who
along with lay members, took professional decisions.   In
general there are good arguments why individual case decisions,
being professional matters, should be considered solely by professionals from the agency, with advisers such as doctors,
psychiatrists, psychologists and so on being co-opted from outside.   Lay people could be encouraged to serve on committees
concerned with matters of general policy and the provision and
allocation of resources.

The financing of the societies' work.

Voluntary adoption societies were almost exclusively dependent on subscriptions and voluntary contributions to carry
out their work.   Repayments authorised by the courts accounted
only for 14.0% of their income.   Only one society received a
very small grant from its local authority.   This left the
societies with the hard task of raising substantial additional
funds.   The most common method was to ask adopters to make
voluntary contributions or sign covenants as 'tokens of their
appreciation of the society's work'.   Almost all adopters
were glad to do so.   Donating money to the society appeared
to take away the element of charity that might be inferred.
Some of the adopters in the sample contributed or covenanted
sums of up to £25 annually.   A number of adopters, however,
wrote back to the respective societies to say that they could
not afford to make fixed and regular payments but would try
and contribute each year according to their financial circumstances.   One serious implication of this practice is the
possible effect it may have on those adopters who wish to
return to the same society for a second or third child.   A
second implication is how far societies may weigh their
selection procedures in favour of their more affluent clients.
A third, is the effect it may have on the relationship
between the child and the adopters who may come to resent
this annual levy, though nothing prevents them, of course,
cancelling the arrangement.

In 1965, the voluntary societies spent an average of
£64 for the arrangement of each placement.   This sum varied,
however, between £46.0 spent by one society to £84.0 spent
by another.   There is no doubt that most of the societies
are functioning under considerable financial stringency.
This partly accounted for the fact that the objectives of
many of them had remained almost unchanged since their inception, and that they were continuing to practise on very
narrow and limited programmes.   In contrast, one of the
wealthier societies, succeeded in introducing new concepts
to its work, defining new needs and objectives and employing a fair number of trained staff.

Many good arguments can be put forward why local authorities should seriously consider grant-aiding voluntary societies. The main one, however, is that the societies are carrying out work that local authorities should be performing themselves. In fact in some areas, social work departments are still channelling a fair number of their own cases to these societies. It is in the interests of local authorities and of the children to develop adequate services in an area because an easily accessible service, and action whilst the child is still young and adoptable, are important factors in adoption work; otherwise many children will run the risk of becoming long-term "care" cases to their own detriment and at considerable expense to the local authority.

The Use of Resources.

The resources available to an agency determine, to a large extent, its objectives and the quality of its practice. It would be misleading, however, to conclude that the amount of resources is the sole arbiter in the situation. In agencies where objectives and programmes are not constantly re-examined and reviewed, additional resources can only be used to carry on with traditional practices and do not initiate change. At the time of the study, most of the societies seemed in danger of reaching this stagnation mainly because of a general failure to carry out continuous reviews and evaluation of their work, and to set new objectives in the light of new needs or new emerging practices. New areas which could have been included were; adequate services to the natural parents; more diverse facilities to enable the placement of unusual children; and experimentation in new selection procedures.

The resources considered necessary to carry out an adoption agency's work satisfactorily are, (in addition to an adequate number of competent staff) suitable premises where applicants and parents can be interviewed and where children may be viewed by would-be adopters; nurseries for short-term care or hard-to-place children; and a ready pool of foster-homes. Our study of practice has shown that the actual use either of nurseries or foster-homes was influenced both by their availability or otherwise, but also by each society's attitude towards the adoption of hard-to-place children and its policy regarding direct or pre-adoption placements. Even if a particular society however, favours direct placements, it will frequently be obliged to make different arrangements for a number of children who, because of either medical requirements or their mother's indecision, may need pre-adoption care. Of 209 children placed by the four societies in the sample, 72 per cent had a pre-adoption placement and the remainder were placed directly. A further analysis by agency showed that whereas all of one society's placements had experienced a pre-adoption placement, in the case of another agency seven out of every ten children were placed directly with adopters. The society that used pre-adoption placements most extensively was the one that had most resources, whilst the society that made the least use, had limited resources, especially in staff. This last society would delay accepting a child's surrender from its mother until the adoptive home was ready to receive it. In the meantime the mother was expected to continue looking after it. The mother would usually be staying in a Mother and Baby Home, but the fact that she had reached a definite decision to surrender earlier, was ignored.

In the case of "hard-to-place" children, attitudes, as well as availability of resources, appeared to influence the extent and quality of the service given. The majority of societies had not developed any special programmes to accommodate the needs of such children. Societies placed approximately only 4.0 per cent of children who were either over a year old or had a physical or colour handicap. Some societies refused to handle the cases of children where the mothers had mentally subnormal relatives; if the mother was taking an unusually long time to make up her mind, in cases where she was described as 'troublesome' or 'hysterical'; if the child was suspected of negroid features or of some physical handicap; and in one case where the child was described as of 'poor' stock. Most of these children were subsequently referred to children's departments but such referrals contributed to considerable ill-feelings between those voluntary agencies and the public agencies. The conclusion could not be avoided that most of the societies concentrated their work on very young healthy infants and had no programmes to accommodate the needs of unusual children.

The social work personnel and their workloads.

The role of the caseworker in an adoption agency is seen as being one that requires skills which are basically similar to the skills of social workers employed in other forms of social work. Besides these, however, some special skills appear to be necessary, such as a high degree of interviewing ability, plus a thorough understanding of human growth and development, marital interaction and normal family life. These skills are connected with supporting and helping natural parents to come to a decision about their child, with selecting adoptive and foster-parents and arranging placings and following them up to see how they are working. The quality and quantity of staff are of crucial importance for the success of any social work undertaking, but especially so in adoption where it is essential that all personnel are trained. The Hurst Committee [17] stressed that there is no other field in which a combination of personality, training and experience is more necessary than in adoption work. The Adoption Agency Regulations, however, do not prescribe any qualifications necessary for caseworkers employed in adoption agencies. The Act simply requires that the staff should be "sufficient, fit and proper". It is left to the registering authorities to interpret these terms. The very wide patterns

observed indicate that the registering authorities give a
variety of interpretations to these terms.

At the end of 1965 the eight societies employed between
them 17 caseworkers, four of whom had a professional training
in social work. Three of the trained workers were employed by
the same society. Four other workers had a degree, diploma or
certificate in social studies but no professional training.
Two of them had only secondary school education and the rest
had allied diplomas and certificates. Unavailability of funds
and the relative scarcity of trained social workers was only
part of the reason why six of the eight societies had no
trained caseworker on their staff. There also appeared to be
a lack of conviction among certain societies about the value
of qualified workers. Because adoption work involves a
fair amount of doing and planning, compared to some other
forms of social work, it more easily gives to the untrained
worker a feeling of achievement and confidence. The anxiety
often experienced in a casework situation is not allowed to
develop because of the amount of planning and activity involved, with tangible results obtained at the end.

There are no agreed standards about what is a reasonable
caseload for an adoption worker to carry. In determining
caseloads in adoption work, account must be taken of time
required to study the child, to complete work with the unmarried mother, in placement and supervision in temporary
foster-homes, selection of adopters, adoptive placement and
supervision in homes. Time needs to be allowed for preparing
reports, travelling, interviewing, telephoning, co-ordinating
with allied professions and attending case-committee meetings.
The geographical area covered and the size of the agency are
additional important factors. Nolt [30] concluded, from her
study on the subject of caseloads, that, under optimum conditions, a worker is able to make one and one half placement
per month. The ratio of staff to children placed, as found
from this study, varied from one worker to every 24 children
to one every 77. The average for the societies was 45 completed placements to each caseworker. The registering authority, that accepted for registration the society that had a
ratio of one caseworker to every 24 children placed, also
accepted the society that had one caseworker for every 77
children. This discrepancy can give the impression that
registration is a mere formality. Though it is considered
advisable to place children at some distance from the homes
of their natural parents, there can be serious drawbacks if
the adoption agency lacks adequate resources to cover a wide
area. One of the societies with the poorest ratio of staff
to cases placed children at distances of up to 150 miles
from its base. Most of the drawbacks connected with this
practice are linked with the difficulty of carrying out
proper enquiries when selecting applicants, and of following
up the placement. In two cases the study came across, one
child was placed in a home in which the husband had a serious
drinking problem and the other with a couple who had just

come together following two separations. These placements were made at distances of 75 to 120 miles from the placing agency's base. The Courts eventually granted the orders, because the alternatives by that time were not very attractive, but they remarked that a local agency making the placement would have found out the circumstances of these two families. Restricting agencies to smaller areas, however, carries the risk of the natural and adoptive parents meeting or of an adopted child marrying a half-brother or half-sister. The present Act gives no protection from such possibility.

Accountability:

Voluntary societies are only formally accountable to the Registering Authority. Following registration, societies must submit annually certain information about their work to the registering authority. The latter has no right, however, to 'inspect' the work of societies. As the Registering local authority may run its onw adoption agency with no better standards being observed, it is arguable whether it is the right body to exercise even the minimal control that Registration implies. Voluntary societies are now entrusted with great authority over and responsibility for the lives of many children and families and it is reasonable that not only should they be registered, but also their work should be 'inspected' by a competent central body.

Consultant Services

Though adoption work mainly consists of a social component, not infrequently the services of consultants from allied fields are necessary. Such professionals as paediatricians, general practitioners, psychologists and psychiatrists, as well as fertility experts may be consulted. A team approach to the problem of diagnosis, selection and placement must be developed. Only one society had developed a team-work approach whilst the rest occasionally used such services, mostly on an ad hoc basis.

II

THE MANAGEMENT AND RESOURCES OF LOCAL AUTHORITY ADOPTION AGENCIES

The 1958 Adoption Act gave explicit powers to local authorities to arrange and participate in the arrangement of adoptions. Before that, they could only arrange for the adoption of children already in their care. No duty, however, is laid on local authorities to provide such services. Adoption work in the local authority was the responsibility of the children's department and is now that of the newly constituted social work departments. Of the 38 authorities replying to our postal questionnaire, only nine had a separate sub-committee responsible for considering matters arising out of the authority's adoption work, and only one had a committee

for approving the final placement. In the remaining ones,
decisions about selection and placement were made either by the
children's officer alone, or solely by the caseworker carrying
out the investigations, in consultation with a senior. The
Hurst Committee [17] condemned the practice by which a children's
officer accepts a child for adoption and arranges for his
placement entirely on his own responsibility. As in the case
of adoption societies, case decisions should preferably be
left to a case-committee composed of professionals.

The Use of Resources

Local authorities are empowered, under the provisions of
the 1937 Children's and Young Persons Act and the 1948
Children's Act, and now of the Social Work Act, to provide a
wide range of services to children who are received into or
committed to their care. Because of this, it is usually assumed that caseworkers in local authority departments, have a
real choice when planning the placing of a child. This study
showed that local authority departments used nursery or foster-
care facilities for one out of every three children they placed,
compared to seven out of ten placed by voluntary societies.
This big difference is mainly explained by the greater number
of direct placements arranged by local authorities compared to
voluntary societies. As with adoption societies, there is
considerable variation in the amount of nursery and foster-care
facilities used by local authorities. Two of the biggest departments in the sample made only minimal use of foster-care
and nursery facilities and preferred direct placements from
the mothers. The indiscriminate arrangement of direct placements often meant a hurrying of the process or expecting the
child's mother to continue nursing the baby until it was six
weeks old or until the adoptive placement was ready. Though
some voluntary societies had a definite policy about pre-
adoption placements which was based on certain concepts and
which eventually determined their use of nursery and foster-
care facilities, no such policy based on any theoretical concepts
was found among the local authority agencies in the sample.
Their practice in the use of resources was mainly determined
by expediency, with a tendency to avoid using a range of
facilities possibly because of their time-consuming nature.

The Casework Personnel and their Workloads.

Only two of the eight local authorities in our sample
employed separate adoption workers. The rest of the authorities did not distinguish between their adoption and other
child care work. Because of the multifarious nature of work
being carried out by the local authority children's department, it was exceedingly difficult to separate the exact
amount of time allocated to adoption work. In looking at
numbers and qualifications, we took the total number of
caseworkers engaged in child welfare work within the eight
local authority agencies in the sample. Of the caseworkers
employed, only one worker in every eight was professionally

trained, whilst half the staff had only secondary school education. Their position was slightly less favourable than that of voluntary societies, but trained staff were generally scarce among both types of agencies. On at least two occasions in 1968, anxieties were expressed in the House of Commons about the training of staff employed in children's departments in Scotland.

The ratio of staff to cases was worked out on the basis of the departments' total child care work, excluding preventive work. The ratio ranged from one member of staff to 39 cases in one department, to one worker to 83 cases in another. The average was one member of staff to sixty-two cases carried. (A study of the workloads of children's departments published recently by the Home Office Research Unit, indicated that the optimum case-load for each worker was approximately 43.)

In view of the high percentage of untrained staff employed by local authorities, as well as the relatively heavy caseloads carried by them, an attempt was made to understand how the workers managed to cope. Part of the answer appeared to lie in theway that most of the departments had organised their work. Almost all the agencies in the sample made constant use of a great number of different forms and of pro-forma letters and reports, designed to meet every possible situation. The only thing left to the caseworker was to fill in the blanks. There were pro-forma letters for communicating with foster and adoptive parents, cyclostyled letters that could be sent to parents, forms which could be filled in with factual information, stencilled curator reports and so on. This massive use of forms did not appear to allow for initiative and flexibility to be developed, but on the other hand ensured that administratively the work was done. As a device it helped untrained staff to carry out administrative functions without being over-whelmed. This tangible doing also creates a feeling of achievement and satisfaction for the untrained staff, comparable with the satisfaction felt by untrained workers employed in adoption societies. Whenever any of the few trained workers dealt with similar cases, they generally followed the same methods and approach as that used by the untrained. There was no attempt to depart from the stereo-typed methods developed by their agencies. This demonstrated not only the power of the agency over the individual, but also that when trained staff were dealing with a type of case that they considered as peripheral to their main activity, they were likely to follow existing patterns of coping, because these were quick and required less thinking and decision making. An individual, however well-trained, seems to stand little chance of influencing his agency's policies and programmes unless supported by many others similarly qualified or unless concerted effort is made at the top to re-examine programmes and to review practices. To initiate change from the top, however, requires a good grasp of the kind of change needed and the principles that may have to be invoked.

Consultant services.

Local authority agencies generally failed to attempt a planned multi-disciplinary approach to their adoption work. Only exceptionally did they use consultative services, though they ensured that such checks as routine medical examinations were carried out. Less attention was paid to the contribution of allied professions in the adoption field, than it was by some voluntary societies.

Conclusion.

The use of resources such as nurseries, foster homes or staff time, was influenced less by their availability or otherwise and more by agency attitudes towards their use or by expediency. The majority of caseworkers employed in both voluntary and local authority agencies were carrying heavy caseloads and had little or no training for the job. A big part of the work was reduced to routine, pro-forma type of activity aimed at meeting legal and administrative requirements rather than designed to suit the special needs of individual cases.

CHAPTER   SIX

ADOPTION AGENCIES AND THEIR CASEWORK SERVICES

TO NATURAL PARENTS

The Adoption Act of 1958 placed no responsibility on adoption agencies to provide casework services to unmarried
parents contemplating the surrender of their children. The
problem of providing services to help unmarried mothers with
feelings and difficulties arising from the adoption situation
was left entirely to the deliberations of each agency. This
situation appeared to be made worse by the absence of any
mandatory requirements laid upon any one statutory agency to
provide general and comprehensive services to this group of
parents. The powers given to local authorities, under the
1948 National Health Act and the 1963 Children's Act, resulted
mainly in a lot of piecemeal action with no uniform pattern.
Because of this, there emerged a considerable division of
responsibility including the blurring of roles and of boundaries which deprived unmarried mothers of continued care at
different stages. Social workers in different types of
agencies accept referrals of cases of unwed parents, only in
so far as they see them to fall within the narrowly defined
function of their respective agencies. If afterwards a
particular client's problem or needs change, she is then
referred to a new agency that is supposed to have a more suitable programme for meeting her new needs. In the course of
this study we came across situations in which unmarried
mothers were referred by their G.P. to the children's department, from there to the Matron of a Mother and Baby Home,
then to the hospital social worker who, on learning that the
mother intended to surrender her child, referred her to a
voluntary society; the latter would re-refer the mother to
the local authority if she suddenly lost interest in adoption
or was vacilating. Each of these workers dealt with only a
small part of the mother's problem and often assumed that
certain other help was either given by the previous worker or
about to be given by the next one in the line.

Adoption agencies are one of many types of agencies whose
work brings them in touch with unmarried parents at the stage
when they are contemplating surrendering their children.
Social work literature generally recommends that good adoption
practice is predicated upon good casework service to natural
parents. A helping relationship with the natural parents, it
is maintained, is essential for successfully initiating and
carrying through the adoption process. At a conference at
Folkestone in October, 1961,[31] the representatives of organisations belonging to the Standing Conference of Societies
Registered for Adoption, resolved that the mother should be
helped by the agency to reach the decision about the baby and
to make the arrangements that are appropriate for her. Also

that the agency should help the mother by giving her as much help and information as possible, concerning both adoption and the alternatives to it. Thus adoption societies themselves see their function, in relation to the natural parents, as going well beyond a formal acceptance of surrender. Helping the mother to make a sound decision about whether or not to place her child for adoption, is accepted as standard practice. Rowe [32] outlines the adoption agency's function with unmarried mothers as being: to help the mother make the best possible provision for the baby's future; and to help her rehabilitate herself, either with or without the child, to become a wiser, more mature person, finding her satisfactions in ways acceptable to our society and enriching, not destructive to herself.

Our evaluation of the agencies' services to the biological parents who surrender their children was based on the following three explicit criteria over which there is general agreement in social work literature:

(i)   the number of actual contacts with the parent(s);

(ii)   casework help given around the adoption situation; and

(iii)   the provision of a background history and background information on the parents.

(i) The Number of Actual Contacts with the Mothers.

Though professional bodies see such contacts as very necessary, they do not lay down rules about any desired number. This is a complex matter which depends on many factors such as the nature of the mother's situation, the stage at which she is referred, what other kinds of help she has already had and whether a husband or putative father is involved. A mother who is conflicted in her feelings and uncertain about her intentions will obviously need more time and more contacts. Likewise, the mother who is referred be fore confinement is more likely to need help over a longer period because she is living through the decision-making process. A mother referred after confinement and who is ready to surrender is likely to need help mainly to reflect on her decision and to try to come to some kind of terms with it. If the contact with the mother is also seen as an opportunity to assist her to rehabilitate herself, then even more interviews will be necessary, and, in the case of adolescents and teenagers possibly a considerable number of contacts will have to be arranged with their parents.

The twelve agencies in the sample placed the children of 376 parents. In just over five per cent of the cases the mother was not seen at all by the placing agency and the surrender was negotiated through another person, usually the Matron of a Mother and Baby Home. In three out of every

five cases the caseworker had only a single interview with the
mother, mainly to arrange surrender and the obtaining of consents. In the remaining cases, two or more contacts took
place.

Local authority caseworkers had a mean of 1.25 contacts
with each mother compared to 1.6 by voluntary workers. The
amount of contact appeared to be mostly determined by the
caseworker's other commitments and the way she interpreted her
role vis a vis the mothers. The occasion when local authority
workers had a succession of contacts with the mothers was
when the child had been in care for some time before it was
released for adoption. The seemingly better performance of
voluntary societies was entirely due to the policy of one
society which continued seeing the mother for as long as she
required help. Out of 71 placements by one society, in 69
cases the mother was either seen once or not at all. Similarly
of 59 placements made by one local authority, only two mothers
were seen more than once.

(ii) Casework Help Around the Adoption Situation.

As stated earlier, the function of the adoption caseworker in relation to the natural parent is rather vague and
unclear. There is, however, one area over which there is general aggreement. This is in connection with help over the
adoption situation, as separate from help in connection with
other personal and social problems that the parent may be
facing. This is an artificial division, of course, as very
often the birth of an illegitimate child and the issues involved are the result of or give rise to a variety of other
problems. For purposes of evaluation, however, we used the
minimum requirements outlined by the profession. These are:
first, that mothers who are referred to adoption agencies
are still likely to need considerable help before they can
arrive at a final decision; some may do so more quickly
than others, depending on the stage at which they are referred. Second, that the mothers will need help in separ-
ating from their child. Third, that they will need help in
resolving, as far as possible, conflicts and guilt arising
out of their decision.

The findings from table 8 show that in over two thirds
of the cases, the contact between the caseworker and the
mother was restricted to the formal surrender of the child
and the obtaining of consents. In these cases, no casework help was attempted concerning the adoption situation
and there was no indication that any of the items, outlined
earlier, were discussed. There was no evidence, from the
content of the records, that the caseworker had an opportunity
to establish, within this contact, the "warm", "understanding"
and "continuing relationship" that social work literature
suggests. This was not surprising, considering that in almost
seven out of every ten cases there was only one contact between the adoption worker and the mother. In the remaining

119 cases (or 31.6%) some kind of casework help was given to the mother in connection with the adoption situation. Two fifths of these cases were, however, handled by a single agency. This was the only agency that had an explicit policy about the extent and type of services to be given to unmarried parent(s); otherwise the help given by the remaining agencies was of a sporadic nature. It could be argued that, in the cases of mothers where the contact was restricted to a formal acceptance of the child's surrender, there was no need for any other kind of help. The pattern, however, established by table 8 suggests otherwise. For instance, in none of the cases handled by independent society was the contact a formal one, whereas in over 90 per cent of cases handled by National society, by Borough II and Borough W, the contact was a very formal and practical one. (Details of the rating system used appears in the main study.)

Table 8. Casework help given to mothers on the adoption situation. (Agency sample N.376)

Agency *	Formal Acceptance of child's surrender	Casework help given by adop. caseworker			Total
		Cons.	Fair	Little	
	N	N	N	N	N
Borough I	7	–	3	1	11
Borough II	35	2	2	3	42
County E	10	1	3	2	16
Borough H	6	–	2	1	9
County H	8	–	3	2	13
County S	5	3	1	–	9
Borough W	54	1	2	2	59
County W	6	–	1	1	8
Independent	–	19	29	–	48
Moral	39	3	4	6	52
National	66	–	3	2	71
Social	21	5	4	8	38
TOTAL	257	34	57	28	376
%	(68.4)	(9.0)	(15.2)	(7.4)	(100)

* Agencies above the black line are local authority ones and those below are voluntary ones.

When the absence of casework help, around the adoption situation, was discussed with a number of casworkers, some referred to the pressure of work but others argued that such help was given either (i) by the Matrons in Mother and Baby Homes or (ii) by the social workers at the hospitals, where the mothers had been confined. As regards (i), Nicholson [34] in her study of Mother and Baby Homes referred to the unresolved arguments between caseworkers and Matrons as to who should give this kind of help to the mothers and remarked that, with few exceptions, the mothers in the Homes were ignorant of the most basic facts about adoption or the facilities they might find helpful if they kept the baby.

Nicholson continues by saying that there was little evidence to suggest that much was done to help mothers with the emotional and practical meaning of their decision, in particular of the decision to surrender the baby for adoption.

To test (ii) i.e. the argument that help on the adoption situation was given by the social workers in the maternity hospitals, we arranged a small comparative study with one hospital. The cases of 38 mothers, who had been seen at four of the twelve agencies in the sample, were followed-up at the hospital where they had been confined. The hospital caserecords were full and detailed and the casework process could be followed through. The casework help on the adoption situation was carefully identified and evaluated on exactly the same criteria as the ones used in evaluating similar help to the 38 mothers at the adoption agencies.

Of the 38 mothers followed-up in this way, only six had some help on the adoption situation by the hospital social workers. At the adoption agencies where the 38 mothers had also been seen, only 12 of them had some form of casework help; the remaining 26 had no help of any kind. Four of the six mothers who received some help at the hospital were also among those who had some help from their adoption worker. Thus, it appears that almost two-thirds of the mothers received no planned help on the adoption situation, either from the hospital or the adoption caseworker. Hospital caseworkers would argue that they do not see that such help falls within their function. They would add that help to the mother to reach a decision and to have opportunities to reflect on it is outside the context of a medical social worker's job, whose main function is to enable the patient to make the fullest use possible of the medical care offered. In other words, the help they give should be compatible with the objectives of the total institution, and that the offer of an adoption service is outside the objectives of a hospital. On the basis of these findings and Nicholson's [34] observations, adoption workers can no longer assume that the mothers receive this kind of help from other workers.

(iii) The Provision of Background Information on the Parents

The provision of an adequate background history of the

parents is considered to be imperative for three main reasons:
(a) to help towards a quick physical and mental assessment of
the child which will enable it to be placed as early as
possible; (b) to provide the adoptive parents with information
that they can later share with the child; (c) to be used as a
diagnostic tool when assessing the parents' needs and planning
around them. Desirable items of information include such
aspects as: the circumstances of the parents' upbrining, aspects of the parents' mental and physical health, the parents'
education and employment record, information on significant
events in the parents' lives, the parents' achievements,
hobbies and interests and the circumstances that led to the
present pregnancy and subsequent surrender.

The overall picture that emerged from the study was one
of striking paucity of information about either of the parents'
backgrounds. In over three out of every five cases, the only
information available was of a factual nature. Information of
a historical and personal type was altogether missing. Only
one of every five cases contained what could be described as
"considerable" information, but two thirds of these were
handled by one single agency. The argument can again be put
forward that the caseworkers handling these cases knew much
more about the mothers' backgrounds than they put on paper.
Though this could be true for certain purposes, it is difficult
to see how this information was for instance transmitted to the
physician who examined the babies. The importance of full
background reports on the parents, reaching the doctor at the
time of the child's medical examination has been the subject
of many conferences and papers. Equally stressed in social
work literature is the importance of building-up relevant information that can be transmitted to the adopters who, it is
hoped, will share it with the child at a later stage. A
current study by the writer on the feelings and observations
of a group of adopted adults is revealing the absolute lack of
information that these persons had about their natural parents.
Both adoption agencies and adoptive parents appeared to collude
in obliterating the child's past. The lack of this important
background information appeared to make these persons feel a
great sense of deprivation, and a big gap in their lives. In
certain instances the adoptive parents were themselves ignorant of basic facts about the child's background.

Contacts with Putative Fathers

In recent years a number of writers have drawn attention
to the needs of the putative father, irrespective of his legal
position vis a vis the child. Such needs are seen to arise
from the fact that he is the father of an illegitimate child
and in many cases of a child that is about to be placed for
adoption. Only one of the twelve agencies in the sample had
a definite policy of pursuing contacts with putative fathers.
This agency had contact with 25.0% of the fathers of children it placed for adoption in 1965. The contact consisted

mainly of one interview and was largely used for the collection of background information and the administration of an intelligence test. In a number of cases the contact was also used as an opportunity to offer help with aspects arising out of the father's relationship with the mother and the surrender of the baby.

None of the remaining agencies attempted to establish contact with putative fathers. Factual information about his age, occupation and physical characteristics was usually obtained from the mother. Most of the voluntary agencies lacked the resources to pursue such contacts, though this could not be said of all public agencies.

How the Mothers were Referred to the Adoption Agencies

Almost half the mothers were referred to adoption agencies by hospital social workers and a quarter by general practitioners. There were more self-referrals to local authority departments than to voluntary societies. External agents, to a great extent, appeared to determine the kind of clients each agency had. From discussions with hospital social workers it emerged that a number of factors influence their decision about whether a mother is referred to one or another agency. Thus, in an area where a particular agency is well staffed, hospital workers tend to refer to them the more complicated cases and refer their more straight-forward ones to agencies that have few resources and are poorly staffed. Another factor is the financial status of the mother. The better off ones are more likely to be referred to voluntary societies because they can afford to meet the required fostering fees. A further important fact, however, is that some hospital workers, influenced by the matching practices of certain voluntary societies, refer most of the better educated type of single mother to them, referring the rest to local authority agencies. In this way, they wittingly or unwittingly reinforce the matching practices of some societies, which use socio-economic background as their main criterion in matching child and adopters. This in turn has created considerable ill-feeling among local authority workers who feel that they are usually left with the less rewarding cases.

Almost half the mothers in the sample were referred to the adoption agencies six weeks, or more, before confinement and only just under a fifth were referred following confinement. Adoption workers attach considerable importance to the timing of the referral, as it affects the time-span available to them to prepare the mother, select adopters and make arrangements either for direct placements or for a pre-adoption one.

Conclusions

The main conclusion to be drawn from this chapter is the great discrepancy between social work expectations and actual performance regarding services to natural parents. Social

work theory outlines a kind of service to natural parents which,
with a number of very interesting exceptions, bears little relation to actual practice. The same gap also exists between
what some agencies profess to do and what they actually do.

Substantial additional resources and a new approach seem
to be needed to enable adoption agencies to widen their programmes to cover not only those parents contemplating adoption
for their children, but all unmarried parents irrespective of
what their decision is likely to be. The boundary lines between a decision to keep and a decision to surrender are so
overlapping, that the continued separation of services to this
group of parents leads both to a waste of limited resources
and to the fact that often real needs are not met.

CHAPTER   SEVEN

AGENCY SERVICES TO THE CHILD

Social work literature outlines certain services for the child that should ensure that he will receive the care he needs and the appropriate home best suited to him. Four areas of careful planning and study are generally recommended under the following headings:-

(i)   study of the child to evaluate his needs and probable capacity to benefit from adoption;

(ii)   the timing of the placement and the provision, where necessary, of temporary pre-adoption care;

(iii)   the preparation and planning of the actual transfer of the child to the adoptive parents; and

(iv)   services for the 'hard-to-place' child.

(i)   Study of the Child to Evaluate his Needs and Probable Capacity to Benefit by Adoption.

This area of study and assessment is separated into two aspects: (a) Study and assessment of the child by the caseworkers; and (b) assessment through an inter-disciplinary approach.

(a) Study and Assessment of the child by the caseworker: A study of the child and of his natural family aims at obtaining information that can be used to assess his physical and personal characteristics, his current development and his special needs. This study should partly determine whether the child is adoptable and the information yield will be shared with the prospective adopters to help them decide about taking him or not. Considering that almost nine out of every ten children were placed before they were seven months old, studies aimed at eliciting certain of the attributes suggested above would be highly restricted. As it is generally agreed that the value of psychological tests for very young infants is very doubtful, the alternatives open to the caseworkers were: to obtain a detailed developmental history, and a family background history. Only one of the twelve agencies in the sample obtained a considerable amount of information about the child's developmental history. The remaining agencies would normally record only some deviation from the range of normal development, such as a physical or mental abnormality or whether it was a non-white child. In the majority of the cases, the records made no reference to the actual child as such, besides such identifying data as name and date of birth. Similarly, in almost two-thirds of

the cases no information was provided on the child's family
background beyond a description of the parents' physical characteristics. On the basis of these findings, apart from a few
exceptions, it would be misleading therefore, to talk of any
organised method of obtaining the child's developmental history and family background as outlined in social work literature.

(b) Assessment through an inter-disciplinary approach: Though
adoption is essentially a social service, the skills and spec-
ialised knowledge of other professions, especially of phys-
icians and, where appropriate, of psychologists and psychiatrists, may be utilised in assessing the child's current development. Recommendations from such assessments will be co-
ordinated by the casework staff, who will then place them,
along with their own final recommendations, before the case-
committee. Of primary importance is the medical examination
of the child before the adoption placement takes place. If
the baby is placed on a fostering basis before it reaches six
weeks old, the medical examination, provided for by the regulations, must wait till then. Besides this rather formal
examination which aims at satisfying the statutory requirements, it is suggested that a medical examination should be
arranged by the agency at an early stage, as part of a plan
for a study and evaluation of the child's needs. For this
purpose, it is suggested that the examination should be made
by a paediatrician, preferably of consultant status, to determine the state of the child's health, his intellectual potential in terms of his natural parents, and also any factors
that may interfere with his development, and their probable
prognosis. Forfar [35] maintains that the worth of the examination is very much related to the type of doctor who carries
it out. It is of crucial importance in examining the infant
to know the past history, the history of any significant illness in the parents or any family history of illness, the
state of the mother's health during pregnancy, the character
of delivery and the state of the infant at birth and subsequently. In this way the social worker sets the stage for
a proper examination. The demands made by this kind of responsible examination point to the need for agencies to liaise
with certain paediatricians in hospitals or local authority
public health departments, who can develop interest in this
type of work and who will in due course develop the required expertise and easily recognise the special needs that
arise in the adoption situation. The examining doctor is
not asked to give his opinion on the suitability of the child
for adoption. Ultimate responsibility for placement, lies
with the adoption agency, provided that the prospective
parents are made fully aware of the child's medical history
and are prepared to carry on with the placement. The Hurst
Committee [17] said that "no provision should be made for the
doctor to express an opinion on the suitability of the child
for adoption. As we have indicated this is a matter for the
applicants to decide when they know the facts." In a few

cases we studied doctors were successful in delaying either
the original placement or the granting of the order.   In
the case of one child the doctor wrote at the end of his
report: " I would not recommend to any of my friends to
adopt this child."   Six months later it was reported to the
Court that the child was doing very well and that the adopters
were very satisfied with its good progress.

Social work literature explains the intensive screening
of the baby as being necessary to make a better assessment of
his needs and not to create unnecessary barriers to his adoption.   The more skilled and experienced the medical exam-
iner, it is argued, the less likely is he to play for safety
and cause unnecessary rejections.   Of the twelve agencies in
the sample only one had a built-in system involving a formal
arrangement with a consultant paediatrician for a detailed
examination based on full background reports.   In some areas
too the shortage of paediatricians had forced agencies to
improvise, but it also meant that the placement of a number
of children was unnecessarily delayed.   The examination
arranged in over half the latter cases was not meant to aid
initial assessment of the child, but to satisfy the statutory requirements.   In a number of cases where the children
were placed before the six week statutory requirement, the
only medical examination took part when the child was already
in the home of the adopters.   This meant again that medical
considerations were not taken into account prior to the
child's placement.   It is also true, however, that the average stay of a child in a pre-adoption placement was longer
where the agency pursued a policy of an intensive medical
screening.

(ii) The Timing of the Placement and the Provision of
Temporary Pre-Adoption Care.

In an earlier chapter it was noted that the use of resources such as nursery and foster-care facilities was only
partly determined by their availability and the number of
staff employed by agencies, being chiefly dependent on the
individual agency's policy regarding direct or indirect
placements.   In recent years there has been much research
into the emotional needs of infancy and childhood and,
though a great deal is still controversial, it is generally
agreed that every child needs continuing loving care from
its parents or parent substitutes.   The lack of this, or
so called emotional deprivation, in the earliest years may
show in severe psychological disorder even in the pre-
school years.   There is a good deal of evidence to suggest
that the child who had had adequate consistent mothering
in the first year or two of life, even if thereafter deprivation has occurred, is likely to make a better re-
covery than the child whose earliest months have been less
satisfactory.   Ribble [36] has also shown that the human infant is born with under-developed brain cells and that the
oxygen needed for the development of his physical and

mental health must be secured through consistent "mothering"
from birth onwards. All these theories have particular relevance for the timing of the child's placement with the adopters and the avoidance, if possible, of unnecessary intermed-
iary moves.

Table 9.   Child's age at placement (Non-related adoptions)
Court Sampe N.783

Age	Vol. Society	Chil. Dept.	3rd Party	Direct	Total
	%	%	N	N	%
3 weeks and under	26.0	30.5	5	9	28.6
4 – 6 weeks	10.0	3.3	2	3	7.3
7 – 9 "	35.0	22.0	2		27.8
10 – 12 "	8.0	15.5			11.0
3 months	5.5	3.0	1	1	4.3
4 – 6 months	10.75	9.5	1	5	10.5
7 – 12 "	2.5	9.0		2	5.5
13 – 24 "	1.0	3.1	1	1	2.2
25 – 36 "	1.0	1.1		2	1.3
3 years and over	0.25	3.0		1	1.5
	100	100			100
N	347	400	12	24	783

(a) The child's age at placement: Almost nine out of every ten
children adopted by non-relatives (table 9) were placed with
their adoptive parents before they were seven months old.
More than a third of the children were placed before they were
seven weeks old but only five per cent were placed when older
than a year.   Third party placements were generally early in
contrast to direct placements which were at an older age.   The
pattern established (table 9), reflects the early and direct
placement of some agencies whilst the majority of placements
of some other agencies only occur between the seventh and
ninth weeks.   The widespread publicity given to the theories
of emotional deprivation, mentioned earlier, resulted in an
apparent effort to place children as early as possible with

their adoptive parents. This influence was evident when we compared children adopted in 1935 with those in 1965. Whilst 90.0% of the children adopted in 1965 were less than seven months old at the time of their placement, this was only true of 65.0% in 1935. Though the trend towards earlier place-ments appears to be in the right direction, the fact emerged from the study that the placing agencies, especially the vol-untary ones, concentrated their work mostly on very young in-fants to the neglect of the older child. Generally, however, all types of agencies placed only an insignificant number of older children most of whom were adopted by foster-parents. It is ironical that the studies in child development may have un-wittingly led agencies, especially voluntary ones, to exclude the older child from their programmes.

(b) Direct and/or Indirect Placements.

Table 10.   Child's moves before adoptive placing
(Agency Sample N. 376)

		N	%
(i)	Foster-care before adoptive placing	175	(46.5)
(ii)	Nursery stay before adoptive placing	25	(6.6)
(iii)	Foster-care and nursery experience	8	(2.2)
(iv)	Direct from their parents to adoptive parents	168	(44.7)
	TOTAL	376	(100)

Just over half the children (table 10) experienced at least one move before they were finally placed with adopters. App-roximately two out of every five were placed directly from their mothers with adoptive parents. After excluding children who were in long term care and nine cases where the mothers took an unusually long time to make up their minds, the remaining 147 children, had a pre-adoption placement which lasted on the aver-age for ten weeks.

Though there is agreement among adoption workers that it is in the best interests of a child to be placed as early as possible with its adoptive parents, there is less agreement about whether such placement should be direct from the mother or preceded by a pre-adoption placement. Three of the agencies in our sample followed a definite policy of not placing any children directly from their mothers with adopters. All three agencies made it a condition to the mother that they would accept her child only if she agreed to a pre-adoption placement and was prepared to meet the expenses. Similarly, they would not accept adopters who insisted on having the child direct from its mother. Such a monolithic policy, though necessary perhaps for some cases, implies that all mothers and all children have similar needs and makes no allowance for individual differences. This practice negates a fundamental social work principle about the individuality of each human situation, which implies that needs should be assessed on an individual basis. Agency time and resources were often used unnecessarily to select foster-parents and arrange placings for children not needing them, and time was also used to pursue the mothers for the collection of fostering fees.

The remaining nine agencies, in the sample, had no policy on the matter and followed a mixed practice. Though these agencies appeared to have a more flexible approach to the matter, this was based less on any principle and more on expediency and practical considerations. Their practice was mostly dictated by the availability or otherwise of resources and their attitude to the use of resources. The indiscriminate policy of direct placements followed by some, meant that there was little effort to distinguish those children and those mothers who needed a pre-adoption placement from those who could be placed directly.

The agencies that had a definite policy of pre-adoption placings explained it on two main grounds: (a) the need to give the mother adequate time to make up her mind; and (b) the medical and psychological requirements.

(a) The need to give the mother adequate time to make up her mind: Agencies that follow the practice of pre-adoption placings for all children on this account assume that all mothers need such a period. The studies, however, by Meyer et al,[21] Yelloly [22] and Triseliotis,[23] as well as retrospective findings from this study, indicate that 70 to 80 per cent of single mothers reach a final decision about the baby within the first ten days after confinement. These findings suggest that, barring other considerations, a high percentage of children could be placed directly from their mothers with the adoptive parents, without having to go through a pre-adoption placement because of indecision on the part of their mother. The studies quoted above, also identified that mothers with certain background characteristics were more likely to reach their decision within this early period. The difficulty which exists with all such predictive studies, is that it is still left to the practitioner to distinguish the mothers who have made a final decision from those who are dithering. This assessment requires considerable relevant knowledge and experience.

The next stage was to get some facts about the

numbers of children who were reclaimed by their mothers at different stages before the adoption orders were granted and how far this was related to the placement being a direct or indirect one. From replies to our postal questionnaire and from the records, it emerged that reclaims amounted to 2.0% of all the placements in 1965. Three quarters of these children were reclaimed before the mothers signed their original consent. Only two children were returned to the agencies by their adoptive parents. Almost an equal number of children reclaimed by their mothers were placed directly and indirectly. The view that reclaims may be related to the single factor of whether the placing was a direct or an indirect one is not convincing in the light of current practice. A factor, which may have as much bearing on reclaims and which no study has as yet assessed, is the process by which the adoption placing is brought about, including the quality and extent of casework service offered to the mother before and after confinement and on the caseworker's diagnostic skills in identifying the mothers who are definite in their decisions from those who are very conflicted in their feelings and likely to change their minds. The figures quoted above are too small to prove or disprove anything. It would be too optimistic, however, to assume that all reclaims will eventually be stopped by following a policy of indirect placements, as this does not take account of the fact that a person's social and personal circumstances can change and can affect attitudes in relation to earlier decisions made. Though the evidence about a definite relationship between age at placement, previous moves and outcome of placement is inconclusive, the few studies available show some relationship between a satisfactory adjustment and an early placement, preferably with no pre-adoption placing experiences. The Child Welfare League of America [37] recommends that some babies can be placed in their adoptive homes directly from the hospital, at the time of the mother's discharge, provided certain conditions have been fulfilled. No study is yet available to show whether it is primarily the child's age at placement which is crucial or whether the determining factor is the diminished likelihood of prolonged early deprivation.

(b) The medical and psychological requirements: The second argument offered, for the need of a pre-adoption placement, is that it is necessary in order that an accurate picture of the child's health and its development can be obtained during this period. Several medical practitioners dispute this need. Karelitz [38] maintains that 95.0% of the babies should be free for placement soon after birth, whilst Bowlby [39] writes: "There is a very serious danger that keeping a baby in a nursery awaiting adoption in the belief that in a few more months an accurate prediction can be made will itself produce retardation, which is then taken as evidence that the baby is inherently backward. So there develops the paradoxical situation in which misguided caution in arranging adoption creates a baby who first appears, and ultimately becomes unfit for it." Dr. Stone in a memorandum to the Joint Committee on Adoption Practices in 1967 wrote: "In view of the possible serious effects of postponed continuous mothering, it is necessary to consider very carefully indeed exactly what postponement is justified on medical grounds." Witmer [40] and her associates reported that in their large Florida sample the incidence of serious disabilities was rare despite the fact that adoptions were independently arranged at an early age and in most cases without testing babies. Whilst it is recognised that some tests and examinations are necessary to exclude any gross handicaps, major hereditary conditions, genetically determined diseases or severe subnormality, medical opinion appears to be moving away from the notion of extensive examinations to present the adopters with a "gilt-edged" baby. Most of the protestations about this practice, and all it implies, have come from doctors rather than from caseworkers in adoption agencies.

The claims of accurate psychological assessments of very young infants, which greatly dominated adoption practice in the forties and early fifties, have now been dismissed in the light of new knowledge.

The actual need for a pre-adoption placement: Of the 208 children in the sample that had a pre-adoption placement, only 95 (or 45.7%) appeared to need it either because the mother required more time to make up her mind, or because of the medical requirements. Well over half of these children had what appeared to be an unnecessary pre-adoption experience which lasted on the average just over eight weeks.

The conclusion seems to point to a need for a change in agency practice that can accommodate the diverse needs of parents and children. A blanket policy of direct or indirect placements does not take account of individual needs. To make such a practice possible, agencies will require more and better qualified staff with access to consultative services. This should make it possible for a quicker and more accurate diagnosis of the situation to be arrived at, followed by the appropriate decision about whether or not the child should be placed directly, with reasons why a pre-adoption placement is necessary.

(iii) The Preparation and Planning of the Actual Transfer of the Child to the Adoptive Parents.

Social work literature and the "standards manuals" of the professional bodies go into great detail about how to plan with care the actual transfer of the baby to the adoptive home. The placement, it is urged, should not be left to chance or done routinely. This is a moment of intense emotional significance and the way the placement is carried out can colour the adopters' whole attitude to the child. While the actual arrangements may differ, in general the placement should be in stages, by offering the prospective adopters the opportunity of hearing about the child, seeing him and only taking him home after opportunities for consideration and discussion. If the child is old enough, it should be helped to participate in the placement and find ways of easing the transition. The warning is again made of the possibility of such placements becoming a routine matter because of the time they consume.

The way the actual transfers were effected, in the sample cases, varied from the well planned to the most impersonal. Two of the 12 agencies had a policy of arranging at least one meeting between the prospective adopters and the baby, before the final placement was made. In such cases, either the caseworkers accompanied the adopters to the Home or Nursery where the baby was, or the foster-mother brought it to the agency's office where it was viewed by the couple. The couple were given the opportunity to hear about the child and its background, to think the matter over, express any possible doubts and discuss their reactions with the caseworkers. The remaining ten agencies had no thought-out policy on the matter. They occasionally asked would-be adopters to go and see the child at the Mother and Baby Home or hospital where it was being cared for, and, if they liked it, to take it home. The caseworkers who knew the natural parents and the baby were often not present, though they would visit the adopters at their home a few days later. In the cases of the few children who were over a year old at the time of placement, no gradual introduction of the child to the family and vice versa was arranged.

Adoption caseworkers, when talking to us, criticised the court procedure for being very impersonal, but often one could describe the transfer of the baby to its adoptive home as an equally impersonal routine and unplanned procedure. The care and planning suggested in social work literature was met only in a minority of cases.

(iv) The Placement of "Hard-to-Place" Children

Social work literature has been urging adoption agencies to give greater attention to, and to allocate more resources to meet the needs of what it describes as "hard to place" children. Such children are thought to be the handicapped, the older child and children of "mixed" blood. A policy geared towards the needs of such children would presuppose not only extra resources in the form of trained social workers, who can concentrate on this group of children, but also more physical resources along with a change of attitude among lay committee members and some adoption workers. There are realistic difficulties in finding homes for these children, but, at a time when adoption is so popular, it is surprising that a greater number of 'handicapped' children are not being placed.

With some individual exceptions none of the agencies had any special programme or had delegated to any member of their staff the explicit remit of finding homes for "hard-to-place" children or for children who might develop into "hard-to-place" ones. The placing of any such children was more by chance than due to any advanced thinking and planning. For instance, of 28 children over twelve months old placed by the children's departments, 25 were already with foster-parents who developed an interest in them.

Our attempt to obtain information and statistics on the number of children that agencies rejected as unadoptable was unsuccessful. Many statutory and voluntary agencies claimed not to keep records of this nature. In another study, which we carried out alongside this one, we came across cases of children who though freed for adoption when a few weeks old, were in nurseries or foster-homes for periods of up to twelve months, before the over-worked staff of an agency could come round to thinking about the children's adoption. By this time, however, the children were too old to be placed with the usual type of adopter, and their adoption was often deferred still further.

No studies are available in Britain to show the extent to which prospective adopters would be prepared to accept a child with some sort of handicap. Maas,[41] from a study in the United States, has found that, of 183 adoptive parents, 61 were prepared to accept a child with a minor handicap, and that 35 of these had children so handicapped placed with them. Twenty-six would accept a child with psychological difficulties, and twelve such were placed; and 63 would accept a child of two or more, 33 of them having received older children. At the court stage of our study, a very small number of children had developed some complication and though the courts suggested postponing the granting of the order, the adoptive parents insisted that they would like to go through as their feelings for the children were unchanged.

Of 783 children adopted by non-relatives, only ten (or 1.3%) were described as suffering from a physical handicap. No child adopted was described as suffering from a mental handicap. The conditions from which the children suffered ranged from the case of the child that had had one kidney removed, to children having slight physical deformities most of which were righting themselves. A further 13 children, of those adopted, had a colour handicap. Ten of these were born to local girls following associations with students from commonwealth countries. Five of the 13 children were placed by a single society. Similarly only one child in every twenty was placed when older than a year and most of these were placed by children's departments with foster-parents who later decided to adopt them. Franklin and Massarik (Child Welfare Nos. 8 and 9, October, 1969 and November 1969) carried out a study in the U.S.A., to shed light on the process and the outcome of adoptions of medically impaired children. They sought to learn how well the traditional objectives of adoption could be reached with this special group of children and parents; and how well parents coped with the added stress of the child's impairment and its social consequences. The research

covered 449 children with a "medical condition" and a control
group of 105 other placements not involving medical conditions.
The authors concluded that for the majority of the study families, the child's medical condition had in no way limited
family functioning nor adversely influenced the parents. The
children were flourishing and leading relatively normal lives.
However, the research workers added that additional help could
well have been used by a small proportion of those in the
"severes" group; in this respect they stress the importance
of a programme of continuing parent guidance for parents in
this group.

In conclusion, either because of the lack of resources
or of suitable adopters, or because of entrenched attitudes,
some agencies still consider it an obligation to place only
perfectly healthy babies and to avoid handling the cases of
older or handicapped children, or of children with a "poor"
background history.

Conclusions

The overall conclusion from this chapter is that better
diagnostic and consultative facilities are needed by adoption agencies, along with a more flexible attitude that can
accommodate the individual needs and circumstances of the
children and their parents. With few exceptions, practice
in this area appears to be dictated either by outmoded
concepts or by expediency.

CHAPTER EIGHT

THE SELECTION OF ADOPTIVE PARENTS

The adoption worker is constantly faced with the difficult task of selecting good families that will provide a certain standard of care for the child in his agency's care. The decision to be made will affect the child's future, the welfare of the adoptive couple and possibly that of the natural parents, as well as the standing of the agency in the community. The adoption worker's job becomes both complicated and uncertain when it is recognised that there is no guide as to what constitutes a good or bad parent and what kind of characteristics need to be looked for in adoptive applicants. Reid,[42] writing on the subject of selection, pointed out that misunderstandings can ensue from an apparent feeling in the community that there are certain essential criteria for parenthood and that adoptive parents should possess these qualities; this in contrast to adoption workers who view their job as being to help adoptive applicants determine whether adoption is the solution for the needs and desires that brought them to the agency and whether they are able to meet the needs of the kind of children for whom the agency needs homes, not whether they will be "good parents". This raises the further consideration of whether adoptive applicants should be viewed as clients needing casework help arising out of their request for a child, or solely as applicants for a child. Both the "investigating" and the "group educative" methods of selection, assume that applicants need some kind of help before they can be entrusted with a particular child. There may be nothing contradictory in investigating applicants whilst supporting them towards better understanding and readiness for adoption. What is perhaps at issue is that the objectives of the selection process need to be well understood by the adoption workers themselves if they are to be shared with the applicants.

The Adoption Act provides no guide about the selection procedure to be followed. The main legal requirement and safeguard is that no infant will be placed by a society, unless the society's case committee has first carried out certain investigations about the adopters. The Hurst committee[17] warned that no arrangements for adoption should be made without a careful preliminary social survey of the adopters, including in particular an assessment of their motives for wanting to adopt a child. It stressed that the crucial stage in adoption practice is the stage of selection and placement. Similarly, Bowlby[39] made the point that knowledge and skill is required in estimating would be adoptive parents and in helping those who are suitable to adjust happily to the intense emotional experience of adopting a baby. He stressed that in this type of work there is no place for the amateur.

From a study of the relevant literature there appear to be four main approaches to the problem of adoptive-parent selection: (i) <u>The administrative method</u>: This method focusses mainly on tangible criteria, such as age, religion and socio-economic circumstances, that can satisfy explicit legal or agency requirements. No investigations are carried out to ascertain the applicants' suitability on less concrete criteria such as motivation or psychological suitability. (ii) <u>The investigative method</u>: This method implies a careful investigation of the applicants based on a series of interviews, preferably by trained case-workers. This method has been considerably influenced by insights from psychoanalysis and dynamic psychology. It bases its study of the applicants on a number of evaluative criteria such as emotional maturity, motivation, knowledge and love of children, strength of marriage and so on. Though it is suggested that the procedure must inspire warmth' and 'confidence' in the applicants, there are indications that it often generates resentment because of the need to ask awkward questions. The process often creates considerable conflict in the caseworkers themselves in that it expects them to inspire 'warmth and confidence' and at the same time assess. In cases of rejection, it can also leave the applicants perplexed as a result of the conflicting cues they received. (iii) <u>The educative group approach</u>: The advocates of this method suggest that, once preliminary eligibility criteria have been satisfied, there should be the workable alternative of accepting all applicants as potential adopters, subjecting them to an educational group process in which they could learn enough about themselves, their motives and needs, to bring them to the stage of deciding for themselves whether they should adopt or not. If they opted out, it is argued, they would still have been enriched by the process of not feeling themselves rejected, and if they decided to remain in the running they would be able to adopt, subject to the agency's decision that they were ready to do so. In spite of its claims, the method cannot do away entirely with the problem of rejection of applicants, but what appears to commend it is that it can be both a tool for selection as well as a preparation for the adoptive role. Though research into the general effectiveness of groups is conspicuously lacking, experience has shown that they tend to become self-selective and by the end of the process those who are left are usually the ones who agree with a certain point of view or outlook. In other words, groups tend to promote sameness rather than the toleration of difference and if exclusively used in adoption selection, they may exclude suitable would-be adopters who never-the-less do not like joining a group. The claim also that unsuitable adopters will voluntarily withdraw is again not borne out by experience in other areas. Adoption caseworkers are also familiar with compulsive couples, where, once they set their minds on adopting, no amount of education or explanation will deter them from wanting to carry on. Attempts to find new methods of assessing adoptive applicants partly arose out of the discomfort felt from carrying authority. The surrendering of such authority is incompatible with the need to safeguard the child's interests. (iv) <u>The scientific method</u>: This method is based on the idea of giving applicants an elaborate questionnaire and the answers being awarded and graded accordingly. The method involves also a battery of personality tests that can identify certain traits or characteristics.

Research has little to offer about the merits or otherwise of the various methods of selection. Until very recently selection was mostly based on methods (i) and (ii), and in the last five years or so, one or two agencies in Britain have been experimenting with (iii). No agency appears to have tried method (iv). In their study on outcome, Amatruda and Baldwin [43] used two groups containing one hundred babies each, one having been placed in the adoptive home by an agency, and the other group having been placed independently. The study found that social agencies arranged better adoptions than the laity. Somewhat different findings were recorded by Wittenborn [44] in a study in Illinois. He found a difference between infants placed by agencies and infants placed independently, which favoured the latter. Independently placed children were slightly superior on some tests. Brenner, [45] in a follow-up study of adoptive parents selected by a single agency in New York graded almost nine out of every ten children as "successful" to "fairly successful". Goldman, [46] in a small study in the Midlands found no evidence to support the view that private or third party adoptions lead to poor matching or to disturbed children. Witmer and her associates, [40] in a follow-up study of independent adoptions in Florida, rated almost two-thirds as reasonably satisfactory and an additional ten per cent "could not be classified as definitely unsatisfactory". Kornitzer [47] in a survey of 500 adopted people, aged five years to 35 and over, found that the success ratings of agency placements were only slightly higher than those of third parties.

No study in outcome has as yet been attempted by taking into account the varied selection and placing practices. Though the overall evidence from studies in outcome is that there is little difference between agency and independent placements, the findings do not invalidate the need for some sort of selection. The closeness in outcome of agency and non-agency placements may reflect the lack of adequate knowledge in this area including the lack of accurate selection procedures. It is an argument for systematic selection and placing practices, followed by evaluation to establish which factors and which methods and procedures contribute to better selection and placings, rather than an argument for no selection at all.

I

ADOPTIVE APPLICANTS

Whatever the arguments for and against certain selection

methods, all the agencies, answering our postal questionnaire, expressed no doubt about the need for selection, though not all of them attached the same importance to the same things. When agencies were asked to say what they look for when selecting adoptive parents, 37 of the 42 gave one or more characteristics or attributes that they expected applicants to have. Five agencies declined to comment or commit themselves. The attribute most frequently quoted as desirable was "stability, maturity and good character" and one of the least quoted was good health. The need for a "secure marital relationship" came fourth in frequency after satisfactory material conditions. Though social work literature suggests ten main attributes that should be evaluated, (to be elaborated upon later in this chapter) the average number quoted by the 37 agencies was 2.3 for each agency. Single attributes such as satisfactory material conditions or general love for children or maturity and stability, were quoted to the exclusion of others.

(i) The number of adoptive applicants: No absolutely reliable figures can be produced to show the number of applicants wishing to adopt each year and it is even more difficult to show the relationship between the number of applicants, the number of children available and the number of those placed. Unfortunately not all local authorities kept complete records showing the number of applications they received and their outcome. The lack of important statistics, so soon after the completion of the year under study, meant that these agencies seemed to attach no importance to planning for the future, or for reviewing their practices.

In 1965, thirty-two agencies in the country had received between them 1410 applications compared to 1121 in 1960. In 1960, however, there were 140 applicants for every one hundred children available, but by 1965 the number dropped to 130 applicants for the same number of children. Fears about the possibility of numbers of infants available outstripping the number of applicants available began to be expressed after 1960 when the rate of illegitimate births rose consistently. Two thirds, however, of the agencies replying to our questionnaire said that they were having no difficulties in recruiting suitable applicants. The remaining agencies were finding some difficulty in recruiting either Catholic applicants or, as they put it, "working-class adopters for boys of a similar background". Though voluntary societies had, in 1965, an average number of 144 applicants for every 100 children available, looked at from the standpoint of individual agencies the situation was very different. For instance, one society had four times as many applicants as children available, whilst three others had only a small excess of applicants over children. Local authority agencies had only 118 applicants for every hundred children available. In areas where there was a clear choice between local authority and voluntary societies, more applicants preferred the latter. Both types of agencies had a drop in the number of applicants per child within the five year period of 1960 to

1965. A closer examination of the figures shows that the narrowing of the gap was due more to an increase in the number of children surrendered than to a decrease in the number of adoptive applicants coming forward. Table 11 shows that though the number of available children in 1965 increased by just over a third compared to 1960, the number of applicants increased by only a quarter. In summary, the study found some evidence indicating that whilst most agencies have an excess of applicants over the number of children available, a minority of agencies had difficulty in recruiting the required number of satisfactory adoptive couples and children had to stay longer in care. In this respect the public is receiving mainly one-sided cues from views expressed by the better known societies which when talking to the press refer to 'baby famine' or limited choices for childless couples to adopt. Such statements, as well as the real fact that these societies reject a great number of couples, appear to put off many would-be applicants. The needs of the children call urgently for the setting up of an adoption exchange bureau to be used by all agencies.

Table 11. Number of children and number of applicants available in 1960 and 1965. (32 Agencies.)

	1960	1965	% increase
Children	800	1078	34.5%
Applicants	1121	1410	25.8%

The various figures suggest that adoption as a method of resolving the problem of childlessness is a minority response. In Scotland only one in every five childless couples proceed to do so. However, as adoption numbers are determined more by the surrendering habits of mothers than the wishes of applicants it would be misleading to draw too many conclusions from this.

(ii) The outcome of applications

In 1965 adoption agencies selected three out of every four applicants compared to four out of every five in 1960. The number of rejected applicants (table 12) was considerably smaller than the number of applicants who withdrew voluntarily. Thirteen agencies that had between three and 16 applicants did not reject anyone, whilst one voluntary agency rejected one every five applicants, the highest ratio in the sample.

The relationship between the available number of children, the number of applicants, the number of homes approved and the actual number of children placed is seen in the next figure. (Fig. 1) This shows that, though the number of applicants to children in 1965 was just over 130 applicants to every 100 children, the homes approved after allowing for

Fig. No. 1.   Number of applications, homes approved and
               placements made per 100 children available
               in 1960 and 1965.

               (Based on the postal questionnaire and
                and the returns of adoption societies)

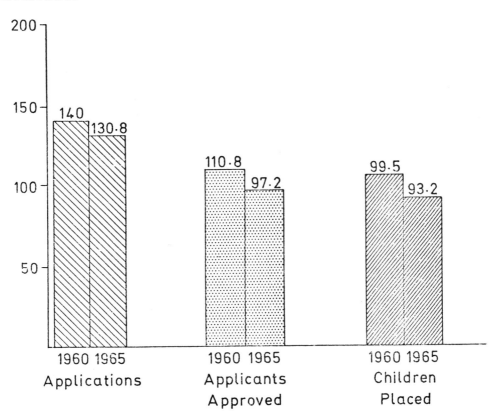

withdrawals and rejections were only 97.2 for every hundred children. In the same year the number of children actually placed was only 93.2 for every hundred available. These figures suggest that some children spent a longer time in pre-adoption placements until suitable homes were approved.

Table 12. Number and outcome of applications
(32 Agencies)

Outcome	1960	%	1965	%
Accepted	886	(79.0)	1048	(74)
Rejected	91	(8)	151	(11)
Withdrew	144	(13)	211	(15)
TOTAL	1121	(100)	1410	(100)

The rejected applicants: Not all rejected applicants were con-sidered as unsuitable. This seemed largely to depend on a particular agency's ratio of children to applicants. Approval or otherwise seemed, to a large extent, to be determined by the margin of applicants over children. Thus 13 agencies that had between 3 and 16 applicants did not reject anyone, whilst one voluntary society rejected a fifth of all its applicants. Of 150 rejected applicants, the biggest number, 44 (or 29.0%) were rejected on medical grounds. One fifth were rejected because of unsatisfactory marital relationships and six per cent on personality grounds. Of those rejected on account of marital difficulties two-fifths were turned down by a single agency.

Applicants who withdrew: Half of those who withdrew did so be-cause they had already got a child from another agency. One in every 8 couples changed their minds, whilst one every six did so because they found themselves expecting an own child. It is a matter of speculation whether the decision to apply in the first instance, represented the resolution of certain psychological difficulties that previously were preventing conception or whether the decision itself brought about such resolution. It can be argued thatamong the general population there may be an equal number of couples who will conceive a considerable time after marriage.

Period between application and placement: The time factor between application and placement is usually influenced by a number of factors, including the agency's method of selection. Agencies which did not insist on elaborate medical certifi-cates and which made little or no use of residential or foster-care facilities tended to have a shorter completion period. Sometimes this period was only a few days. Agencies

that had fewer applicants per child, also tended to complete
their studies and placements within a shorter period. The
average waiting period between application and placement for the
twelve agencies in the 'agency sample' was seven months. Eight
out of every hundred applicants had a child placed with them
within a month after applying and forty out of every hundred
had a child in less than three months. No clear pattern of
practice emerged from any of the twelve agencies, but one
agency that followed certain study procedures, rarely placed
a child in under six months. This agency would first review
an application and decide whether it satisfied the agency's
eligibility requirements; if yes, arrangements and appoint-
ments to have the first and subsequent meetings were made
depending both on the caseworker's and the applicant's other
commitments; references were taken up and medical certificates obtained; preparing a final report for the case
Committee would be prepared; if approved, liaison with another worker would take place to find a 'suitable' baby for
the applicants; arrangements would be made for the applicants
to see the baby; applicants would be allowed some time to
make up their minds before the final placement. It was not
surprising to find that all these activities took between
six to seven months. For the remaining agencies, the timing
of completion was mostly determined by pragmatic considerations. This appeared on the surface as flexible practice,
but in fact it led to some very quick and hasty placements
without adequate selection or preparation. In one particular case the adopters were themselves surprised when, within
two days after they had met the adoption worker they received
a telephone call to collect a baby from a hospital "if they
liked it". The delays for 96 applicants who had a child
placed with them nine months or more after they applied to the
agency, were due to: lack of agency time (43%); awaiting
medical reports (19%); no suitable child available (19%);
waiting for references (11%); temporary change in the applicant's circumstances(8%).

The overall findings suggest that some agencies can
quicken their studies whilst some others can spend more time on
them. It is recognised, however, that the need to speed up
enquiries, to avoid keeping applicants in anxious suspense,
conflicts with the need to establish their suitability.

II

THE INITIAL PROCESS — ESTABLISHING ELIGIBILITY

Agencies required of all adopters, as a first step, to
fill in a form to establish themselves as applicants. The
form asked for certain factual information such as names, address, date of birth, date of marriage, religion, occupation,
sex, age preference etc. Agencies used this information for
a preliminary sorting of applications and for the rejection of
those who did not meet basic requirements. This process is

meant to save agency time and also it avoids raising unnecessary
hopes in the applicants. Each agency had its own eligibility
criteria which appeared to determine, at application stage,
whether the next step should be further study of the applicants
or rejection. Many of these criteria had been arrived at by
the individual agencies with no regard to requirements by other
agencies and with no regard to current thinking and knowledge.
They often reflected either past thinking about adoption practice and human development, or the attitudes of the organiza-
tion under whose auspices the agency was functioning, or in
some cases they simply reflected the individual caseworker's
understanding of, or hunches, or prejudices about, what requirements should be met. Some of the requirements acted as a
kind of rationing system and were often changed in the light
of fresh developments or such practical considerations as the
supply and demand for babies. This lack of uniformity in requirements appeared to offer the would-be applicant a real
choice and an opportunity to shop around the various agencies,
but it had also its dangers in that no consistency could be
maintained. A change of worker could result in a change of
some of the eligibility requirements. A flexible approach at
a time when little is known about the relative merits or otherwise of particular requirements is certainly desirable, but
this should reflect available knowledge on the subject, as it
then has an in-built possibility of changing and developing
with the increase of knowledge. At the moment, agencies that
are rejecting applicants, mostly at enquiry stage, on such
factual aspects as age, years after marriage, religious beliefs and so on, are negating fundamental social work principles about the individuality of each human being. Such
individuality cannot be judged on single attributes whose
prediction value is, to say the least, doubtful.

(i) Consideration of legal requirements: The selection process
begins by eliminating those not meeting the legal requirements. Applicants must be domiciled in England or Scotland
and generally reside here if the order is to be made here.
There are exceptions for those not ordinarily resident in the
country. The Act also provides for a minimum age limit for
adoptive parents, but it makes no reference to an upper age
limit. Also, if husband and wife do not adopt jointly, they
cannot adopt separately without the other's consent. Adoption
agencies are also expected to eliminate at selection stage
the type of applicant from whom a child might have to be removed under a "place of safety" order. Criminals and drunk-
ards could obviously come into this category.

(ii) Application of eligibility criteria. As stated earlier
on, adoption agencies have a latitude of operation and, apart
from the few legal requirements to which they have to conform, there are no other restrictions in operating their
own eligibility requirements.

(a) Age of Applicants: Adoption agencies were found to have
a variety of age limits for applicants. A third of the
agencies said that they had no upper age limit. The chances

of a couple over forty being accepted depends on which agency
they apply to and this in turn may be determined by the area
where they happen to live. Local authority agencies appeared
to be more flexible compared to voluntary ones. None of the
agencies, however, held absolutely to their professed age requirements, especially when selecting homes for "hard-to-place"
children.

Table 13.   Age of non-related adopters at placement
(Court Sample – Mothers N. 783 Fathers N. 779)

	Ad. Mother			Ad. Father	
	N	Y		N	Y
Under 25	54	(7)		10	(1)
25 – 29	192	(25)		113	(15)
30 – 34	291	(37)		226	(29)
35 – 39	174	(22)		238	(30)
40 – 44	51	(6)		144	(19·)
45 and over	21	(3)		48	(6)
	783	(100)		779	(100)

The age of non-related adopters ranged at placement between 23 and 57 years. Almost seven per cent of mothers
(table 13) were under 25 at placement, whilst one in every
eleven were forty or over. The mean age of adopting mothers
was 32.1 and of fathers 34.5. A higher rate of mothers over
forty were adopting for the first time, and a higher rate of
mothers under 25 were having a further child. Of those adopting at the age of forty or over, almost three quarters
married when thirty or over. In their case it looked as if
the prospects of an own child were poor at marriage. Fertility in women, according to various experts, begins to
diminish after the age of thirty and declines more sharply
after 35.

Available studies on the effect of the adopters' age on
adoption outcome are inconclusive. The majority view appears
to be that age by itself is not a significant factor, though
the placing of children with very young and with very old
couples involves greater risks. Age by itself is an arbitrary
factor as a criterion for selection, as people do not mature
at the same rate either physically or emotionally. Agencies

in general seek couples who are not too young, able to realise
the implications involved in adoptive parenthood, and not too
old, running the risk of death or incapacity before the child
is sufficiently independent.

(b) Marriage and Family Structure

Marital Status: Over one third of the agencies, replying to
our questionnaire, said that they would consider a remarried
couple, one or both of whom had previously divorced, but two
out of every five indicated that they would not. In actual
practice there were only five (or 0.6%) adoptions by couples
falling into this category. All five placements were arranged
by local authority agencies and three of the children were in
the authorities' care. Four out of every five agencies will
not consider widows or spinsters which reflects the belief
that every child should have the benefit of a family with both
parents. The courts granted 1.4% of orders in favour of such
women, two thirds of whom were related to the child. The majority of these adoptions were for children who had been placed
first on a fostering basis. The motives of local authorities
in pursuing such asoptions were far from clear. Financial
and emotional support by the visiting child care worker were
withdrawn after the orders were made, in spite of considerable
evidence that such support was still necessary. The local
authorities could perhaps claim that these children were
successfully rehabilitated. This comment is not an argument
against single-parent adoptions as such, but rather that,
where necessary single parents with at least the relative
emotional and material propensities should be selected, sub-
sidised in special circumstances, and supported on an on-
going basis. The arrangement need not be on the traditional
adoption type but a form of guardianship.

Adoptive parents' age at marriage: Age at marriage is one of
the most important determinants of family size. A late
marriage, for instance, can act as a barrier to reproduction
and adoption may be one of the solutions for the couple who
are motivated to rear a child. Childless adoptive mothers
in our sample generally married at an older age compared to
fertile mothers in the general population. Though at this
period three out of every four spinster women were marrying
when under 25, only half the adoptive mothers did so. At
the other end, whilst only one in every ten women were
marrying when thirty and over, among the adoptive mothers
the rate was one in every five. The average age at marriage
of spinster women in the areas covered by this study was
23.4 but that of adoptive mothers was 25.2. Further differences in age appeared when the age-group of adoptive
mothers was analysed by social class. This showed that the
lower the social class background of the mothers the younger
they married, in contrast to those of higher social class
background who married at an older age.

Length of marriage: Two thirds of the children had adoptive

parents who had been married from five to nine years when placement occurred, and a quarter had parents who had been married
ten or more years. Only one in every ten children were adopted
by couples who had been married for less than four years.

The mean number of years between marriage and the placement of a first child was 7.1. This period is considerably
longer than the average period taken by a family among the
general population before they have their first biological
child. The delay of adoptive parents before they have their
first child appears to be due less to agency requirements than
to the long period that couples take before they reach their
decision. Some couples do not appear to try for a baby soon
after marriage and by the time they discover their handicap
considerable time has elapsed. However, in the case of certain groups of adopters such as those marrying when over 30
and those of lower socio-economic background, the delays appeared to reflect agency requirements and the applicants' esti-
mate of themselves regarding satisfactory material standards.

Of the agencies replying to our questionnaire, over one
third said that they had no minimum years' requirement between
marriage and adoption. One in every four agencies, however,
stipulated five years and one agency in every three required
a minimum of three years. In actual practice all agencies
occasionally placed children with couples outside their professed minimum period. The insistence of many agencies on a
three year period appears to be connected with the belief
that this is a testing stage for the stability of the
marriage.

In summary, the average adoptive mother gets married at
a later stage compared to the general population and has her
first child at a much later time compared to biological
mothers. The lower their socio-economic background the
younger they married, but it took them more years after
marriage before they adopted. The converse was true of
couples of a higher socio-economic background: they married
older but adopted within a shorter period following marriage.

(c) Religion: Religious requirements by adoption societies
have occasionally provoked strong reactions from would-be
adopters. As a considerable number of societies are denominational, they have a vested interest in promoting adoptions
only with couples of a similar religious affiliation. All
sectarian agencies required formal church affiliation and
some of them evidence of regular church-attendance. Some
applications were held back to give time to vicars to observe the religious habits of a number of applicants. Non-
denominational societies too appeared to be equally influenced by religious considerations and this attitude was responsible for barring a number of couples from adopting. It
was expected that the setting up of local authority agencies
in 1958 would make it easier for couples professing no religious affiliation to adopt, but by the mid-sixties a
number of individuals in England felt it necessary to set up

the Agnostic Adoption Society. Most local authority agencies
stipulated to us that they were prepared to consider applicants
professing no religion, but three agencies would not consider
them. In the case of the latter, the requirement was not decided upon by their respective committees but represented the
views and requirements of the individual children's officers.
One children's officer remarked that there was no point in considering such applicants when there were plenty of otherwise
"suitable" applicants to choose from. On the whole, local
authority agencies were found to have less religious bias
compared to adoption societies, but individual workers occass-
ionally set up their own criteria in this matter. In the
whole sample we did not come across a single adopter who had
not declared a religious affiliation. Sectarian groups appear
to exercise considerable control over the adoption market by
the sheer fact that they exist and offer a kind of service.
There is no evidence from research to support a positive
correlation between strong religious affiliation in adoptive
parents and good adjustment in the child.

(d) Aspects of Fertility and Childlessness:

Gough [48] writing in 1959 remarked that it used to be
thought that adoption casework was the one field in which the
client did not come to the worker with a problem. "It is now
seen", he added "that they now come with a very real problem
that of childlessness, absolute or relative." Humphrey and
Ounsted [49] found that one fifth of the couples whose adopted
children were referred for psychiatric treatment had lasting
preoccupations with their failure to have children. Kirk [50]
looks at the problem of childlessness as one of role handicap; he sees the wife as being the more deprived because her
roles as a child-bearer and child-rearer have been "mutilated"
in childlessness but that these can be partially restored in
adoption. The husband's handicap is his being deprived
mainly of the opportunity to provide consanguine members of
the kinship . Responsibility for childlessness can give
rise to diverse reactions among the marital partners and
these may occasionally be voiced at the selection interview.

Investigation of childlessness: Childlessness is a symptom
of various conditions and not a diagnosis. The reasons for
which couples may be childless vary. Some may even choose
to have no children whilst some others may have had several
unsuccessful pregnancies. As there is a feeling that it is
not "fair" for an adopted child to go to a family where
there is a possibility of further children, we asked agencies
to say whether they ask applicants to present evidence of
sterility and/or infertility tests. Only two societies said
they require evidence of medical investigations. Both
societies that require such evidence, in practice placed
some children with families that subsequently gave birth to
an own child. Of local authority agencies, one fifth required proof of such investigations.

From the records of three agencies that kept notes on

the circumstances of each couple's childlessness we were able
to identify the reasons for their childlessness. These findings show (table 14) that the number of women diagnosed as in-
fertile was slightly higher than the number of men similarly
diagnosed.

Table 14. Responsibility for childlessness
(Based on the records of 3 of the twelve
  agencies in the sample)

	N	%
Wife's infertility or subfertility	20	(21.7)
Husband's infertility or sub- fertility	16	(17.4)
Miscarriages, still births, etc.	26	(28.2)
Both parents normal	21	(22.8)
No attempt to establish cause	9	(9.8)
TOTAL	92	(1 00)

Though there is no evidence to support the view that the
placement of a child helps a couple to overcome their in-
fertibility, many couples who apply to adopt, do so in the
hope that they will eventually conceive. This in itself de-
monstrates the difficulty many couples have over accepting
their situation without any lingering hopes. Such hopes
should not be a bar to adoption unless the pre-occupation
lingers-on undiminished. In the latter case an over-
idealisation of natural parenthood has many similarities with
the adopted child's over-idealisation of his natural parents.

How big a family: Sixteen per cent of the non-related adoptions were by couples who had one or more of their own children. Another 30 per cent had previously adopted one or more
children and only just over half of the couples were first adopters. It is difficult to judge whether the number of
couples who adopt a second or third child (30.0%) is a big
enough rate to justify the comment that adoption tends to become more popular with people who have actually experienced
parenthood, or to wonder why more couples do not proceed to
adopt more than one child. The latter, however, is a more
complicated issue because of the hitherto limited number of
babies available.

Witmer et al, [40] writing on the outcome of adoptions in
families with own children, claim that the lower average
ratings, where there were own children before adoption, were
not the direct result of mixing own and adopted but that one

factor involved was that such parents were likely to be older at the time of the placement of the adopted child. In general, however, the various studies suggest that what should be evaluated at selection stage is the emotional attitudes prevailing in the home and not the presence or absence of other children.

Choice of Sex: Various writers have suggested that where applicants had a definite sex preference, they predominantly wanted a girl. Sex preference in adoption has been looked at from various points of view, such as the "narcissistic" concern of women in preferring a female child, or that the female child is a symbol of affection, and even more that it costs less to raise a girl than a boy. A preference for boys has been associated with male preference to carry on family consanguinity. Cultural factors as well as fashion cannot be ignored either. Sex preference in adoption cannot be divorced from the surrendering habits of biological parents. The fact that more boys were adopted in Scotland (52.2% in 1965) is related to the fact that natural mothers tend to surrender fewer girls than boys. As regards choice by adopters, it is misleading to study adoptions in general and a better guide is to study sex preference for a first child. Our study showed that in expressing preference for a first child, one third asked for a boy, 28.2 per cent asked for a girl and the remaining 38.5 per cent expressed no preference. Those who expressed no preference were more likely to get a boy than a girl. It is very possible that some of those who expressed "no preference" were either afraid of prejudicing their chances or were hoping to get a second child and so in the latter case, preference for a first child was less pronounced. The previous assumption that adopters prefer girls to boys, is not borne out by facts - at least as far as first adoptions are concerned. It has also been assumed that couples adopting a second or third child, would prefer a child of the opposite sex to the one(s) they already had. In fact, almost a third of those who adopted a second child chose one of the same sex as the one they had. There was a greater tendency, however, to adopt a second girl than a second boy.

(e) The Health of Adoptive Applicants

The Adoption Agencies Regulations do not require of agencies to obtain medical certificates on the applicants' health, but most agencies ask for a medical certificate during the selection stage. This is to ensure that medical implications will not bar the applicants from adopting at the court stage. When the petitioners lodge their application to the Court, they are required to attach a certificate on a prescribed form and signed by a medical practitioner, usually the family doctor. This pro-forma certificate does not allow for any detailed information to be inserted and the only expectation is a generalised statement.

Half of the agencies in the sample, had no particular policy on the matter of medical certificates. Sometimes they would ask for them before the placement but very often no

certificate would be asked except after the child was placed.
The certificate would then be attached to the petition submitted
to the court. This meant that aspects of the applicants' health
were not considered at the selection stage. The remaining
agencies would always ask applicants to consent to a medical report on a form specially drawn up by the agency. The form was
forwarded by the agency to the applicants' doctor and the latter
was expected to examine the applicants and report to the agency
whether the couple suffered or were suffering from a number of
specified diseases, including psychiatric conditions. Where
the medical reports indicated that there were health problems,
the agencies would occasionally, but not always ask the same
doctor to elaborate on his report. Where the reports were not
unreservedly favourable, at least two agencies would ask for
further medical advice as to future risks. Because of the
different types of certificates reaching agencies and courts,
considerable omissions were found in the certificates going to
the courts, compared with those going to the agencies. Many
medical conditions, that were originally included in the certificates obtained by the agency, were not included in the
ones lodged with the courts. The explanation may be connected
either with the general layout of the prescribed official
certificate or with the fact that the court certificate was
personally obtained by the applicants from their doctor. In
one administrative area the medical certificates that went to
the courts quoted 16 of 128 applicants as having suffered or
as suffering from some sort of disease and only one applicant
was quoted as suffering from a psychiatric condition. Of the
certificates that went to the adoption agencies for the same
128 applicants, 49 of them were described as having suffered
or as suffering from some kind of disease. Eleven of these
conditions were connected with a psychiatric disturbance. In
one case the adopting mother had a prolonged period of de-
pression and in two other cases the adoptive fathers had been
under psychiatric treatment for at least five years. There
were four cases of chronic anxiety.

Local authority agencies selected double the number of
applicants who suffered or were suffering from some kind of
disease, than voluntary societies. Certain psychiatric and
physical conditions could have merited further consideration
with advice from a medical consultant, before a final decision to place the child was reached. The somewhat perfunctory scrutiny of the applicants' health contrasted with the
more detailed scrutiny of the infant before placement and
before the granting of the order. The study came across
two distressing situations which came to light only at the
time of granting the order.

(f) Socio-economic Background of Adopters

The findings (table 15) confirm the commonly held view
that the two upper social classes are over-represented in
adoption, whilst the opposite is true of the two lower
classes. Voluntary societies selected more applicants from
the two upper classes and less from the lower classes. The

Fig.2. Comparison by area of adopters' socio-economic background.

(Court Sample)

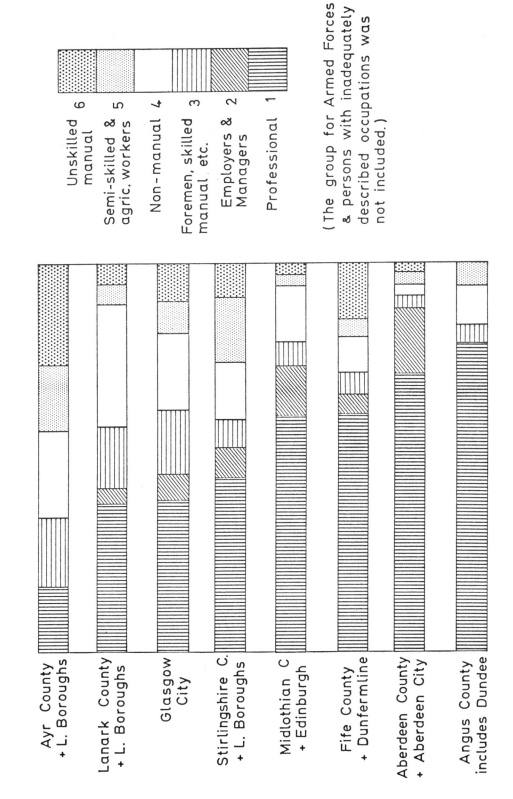

6 Unskilled manual

5 Semi-skilled & agric. workers

4 Non-manual

3 Foremen, skilled manual. etc.

2 Employers & Managers

1 Professional

(The group for Armed Forces & persons with inadequately described occupations was not included.)

Ayr County + L. Boroughs

Lanark County + L. Boroughs

Glasgow City

Stirlingshire C. + L. Boroughs

Midlothian C + Edinburgh

Fife County + Dunfermline

Aberdeen County + Aberdeen City

Angus County includes Dundee

contrary was true of local authority agencies. (It should be remembered that this choice does not exist in all parts of the country.)

Table 15.   The social class background of adopters
(Court Sample N. 783)

	Voluntary Societies		Local Authority		Total	Census 1961
	N	%	N	%	%	%
I – Professional	80	(21)	33	(10)	(15.7)	(3)
II – Intermediate	97	(25)	62	(19)	(22.2)	(13)
III – Skilled	179	(46)	165	(50)	(48.0)	(51)
IV – Partly Skilled	24	(6)	47	(14)	(9.9)	(23)
V – Unskilled	7	(2)	23	(7)	(4.2)	(10)
	387	(100)	330	(100)	(100)	(100)
Non-classifiable	13		17			
TOTAL	400		347			

A further analysis of these figures by occupation, showed that the couples who adopt from the two upper social classes are mainly professional people such as doctors, teachers, solicitors, architects, electrical engineers and others similarly qualified professionals. Employers and managers formed only a small percentage of adopters compared to their numerical strength and even to their material wealth. Why adoption appears to be more popular among professionals and less so among employers and managers may again be related to attitudes about inheritance, fears of unknown heredity and perhaps to the lingering feeling that adoption is only for the working classes. The professionals, who were mostly graduates, possibly represented a more enlightened section of the community. Similarly, just under half of those classified under 'skilled' occupations, were non-manual workers such as, insurance officers, bank clerks, salesmen, etc.

A further significant difference was the variation of the socio-economic background of adopters in different parts of the country (Fig. 2) After taking into account the different population structure as well as the numerical representation of each socio-economic group, in each area, a varied pattern emerged which showed that in the Eastern part of the country, far more professional people adopted than in the Clydeside conurbation and the Western part of the country. The main explanation for this is that, in the latter part of the country, adoption is still looked upon as a mainly working class institution which is only gradually spreading among the lower middle-classes and less so among the upper classes. It thus appears that in some parts of the country there are still many untapped potential adopters. In the event of general scarcity of adoptive applicants, an educational campaign aimed at reaching this area as well as certain occupational groups in the community could prove rewarding.

(g) Housing

In the areas covered by the study the average number of owner-occupiers was 27 per cent, whilst the average number of owner-occupiers who adopted was almost double this rate. These figures reflect again the number of middle-class famil-ies adopting, but equally 45 per cent of those in social class III were also house or flat owners. These figures suggest that adoption is an institution which is increasingly entered into by the upward aspiring section of the community.

(h) Couples Adopting "Hard-to-Place" Children

This group comprised a total of 64 couples who adopted an equal number of children who could be described as "hard-to-place." Fifty-two of the 64 children had been in the care of local authorities. Couples adopting these children (mostly foster-parents) appeared to differ considerably from couples adopting other children (table 16). Couples adopting hard-to-place children differed from the remaining ones in the sample by being older, of lower socio-economic background, having more own children, a greater percentage having suffered or suffering from sone kind of disease, a smaller percentage owning their own houses and finally the few spinsters and wi-dows that featured in the sample, were mostly confined to this group of children. There was one exception to this, in that the few couples adopting children of "mixed" blood were mostly of a higher socio-economic background. Though the numbers were too small for many conclusions to be drawn, these adopters were mainly professionals who appeared to be more enlightened and possibly had less reservations about adopting a coloured child.

The findings from table 16 suggest that, in the case of hard-to-place children, agencies compromised considerably in their expectations of adoptive applicants. It is difficult, though, to say how far these could be described as "marginal" couples adopting marginal children. At least one agency, however, would not consider applicants from a lower socio-economic background unless they were prepared to consider an 'unusual' child initially on a fostering basis, with the possibility of adoption in the future. Such an approach

Table 16. The characteristics of couples adopting "hard-to-place" children compared to the rest of the adopters.

(Court Sample N. 748)

	Age 40 & over	Age under 25	Ad. Mother's status Single/Widow	Social Class I+II	Social Class III	Social Class IV+V	Fam. composition other children Own	Fam. composition other children Adopted	Health present or past illness	Housing Owner
	%	%	%	%	%	%	%	%	%	%
(a) In care and colour group:										
(N.51) "White":	33	11	17	14	54	32	40	17	19	27
(N.13) "Coloured":	33	10	-	60	40	-	50	20	10	40
(b) Rest of Adopters: (p.684)	8	7	0.3	36	46	13	14	29	11	54

Table 17. Summary of agency eligibility criteria (Agency Sample – 12 agencies)

	Upper age limit for wives				Marital status			Yrs after marriage				Relig-ious require-ments	Fertil. tests re-quired	Own child-ren accep-ted
	40	45	50	No limit	re-mar.	wid.	sing.	3	5	7+lim.	No lim.			
Borough I	–	–	–	Y	Y	N	N	–	–	–	Y	N	Y	Y
Borough II	–	–	–	Y	Y	Y	N	–	–	–	Y	Y	Y	Y
County E	Y	–	–	–	P	N	N	Y	–	–	–	N	N	Y
Borough H	–	Y	–	–	P	P	N	Y	–	–	–	N	N	Y
County H	–	–	–	Y	P	P	P	–	–	–	Y	N	N	Y
County S	Y	–	–	–	P	N	N	Y	–	–	–	N	N	Y
Borough W	–	–	Y	–	P	N	N	–	Y	–	–	Y	N	Y
County W	–	–	Y	–	N	P	N	–	–	–	Y	N	N	Y
Independent S	Y	–	–	–	Y	N	N	Y	–	–	–	N	Y	Y
Moral S.	–	–	–	Y	N	P	P	Y	–	–	–	Y	N	Y
National S	–	Y	–	–	Y	N	N	–	Y	–	–	Y	N	Y
Social	–	–	Y	–	N	P	N	Y	–	–	–	Y	N	Y

Key to symbols: Y = Yes

N = No

P = Possibly or occasionally

suggests the application of criteria of less eligibility towards applicants from less favoured social backgrounds. The
practice also implies that the applicants' wishes to become
adoptive parents are not properly respected.

Summary:

     A great variety of eligibility criteria are used by
agencies in the process of selecting adopters. (Summary
table 17) This variety could have been viewed as a sign of
flexibility and health, except for the fact that only in a
minority of cases were these criteria worked out and formulated
into practice-principles. For the majority of agencies the
criteria represented the views, principles, personal beliefs
and prejudices of individual workers or committees. In spite
of this, there has been evidence of some movement away from
rigid attitudes in certain factors such as upper age limit,
the presence of own children in the family, fertility tests
and number of years after marriage. No effort has been made
yet to collate the eligibility requirements of the different
agencies and publicising them so that would-be adopters
could see where their special needs could best be met, thus
avoiding embarrassment and unnecessary dependency.

III

THE   STUDY   PERIOD   PROPER

     Most of the requirements that determine initial eligib-
ility are usually supplied at intake stage. If the agency is
satisfied, the applicants will then go on to the next stage,
the study period proper. The investigating method generally
used by social workers for the study of applicants, involves
a series of interviews which aim at establishing each applicant's personal suitability. The caseworker is expected to
assess general suitability for adoptive parenthood, including
the quality of emotional relationship the applicants can
offer to an adopted child. Rowe [33] comments that "home finding
for adoptable children includes studying adoptive parents so
that their personalities, attitudes and life situations can be
understood and the most suitable family chosen for each child."
Though greater flexibility in selection is urged now than was
the case fifteen years earlier, social work literature and
writings in child development stress the need for a careful
study of the psychological factors involved, to enable an in-
formed decision to be reached in the end. The United Nations
report and the Hurst Committee stressed that high importance
should be attached to the applicants' motivation as it is probably the most decisive element in the success or failure of
adoption. It is maintained that adoptive parents are usually
moved by a great variety of motives of which they may or may
not be conscious themselves, but that it is the caseworker's
responsibility to understand and assess them. Others warn,
however, that motives should be understood in terms of the
applicants' total personality. Ripple [51] claims from her

follow-up study of adopted children that there is little relationship between factors considered in adoption family studies
and outcome of adoptive placement. It was found that such
factors as marital interaction, motivation for wishing to adopt,
socio-economic factors, feelings about childlessness etc.,
which have seemed important to adoption agencies had little
relation to outcome. Ripple suggests turning our attention to
the placement process rather than putting so much effort into
"evaluating"the family. It is recognised that, if the assessment is going to carry some degree of authority and objectiv-
ity, both knowledge and experience are required on the part of
the caseworker. It is assumed that trained workers have a
common body of knowledge to which they usually refer and that
they evaluate behaviour and aspects of information they receive, against this particular background. Untrained workers,
however, have to rely mostly on their experience, though experience by itself can be of limited value unless examined
and re-assessed by its effectiveness in practice. In fact
experience alone could easily lead to a repetition of past
mistakes and to the perpetuation of traditional practices.

The aim of this part of the study, was to examine the
factors that entered into the caseworkers' assessments of the
adoptive home, the sort of information and criteria used in
reaching decisions about the suitability of applicants, and
how far these reflected the criteria outlined by the social
work profession. Social work literature stresses that without neglecting environmental and material factors, the
selection decision ought to be influenced mainly by information about the psychological and emotional make-up of the
applicants and by information about their attitudes to certain
matters. From social work literature and the standard
manuals of the various professional bodies, the following factors were identified around which, it is suggested, basic information should be obtained:

(i)   total personality of the applicants;

(ii)   their emotional maturity;

(iii)   the quality of their marital relationship;

(iv)   their attitude towards childlessness and infer-
         tility;

(v)   their understanding of children and their needs;

(vi)   their attitude towards illegitimacy and unmarried
         parenthood;

(vii)   their emotional motivation;

(viii)   housing situation; and

(ix)   socio-economic circumstances.

The above standards, suggested by the profession, were
used as evaluative criteria. (It was not the intention of this
study to examine the validity or otherwise of these standards.)

We are aware that we are using somewhat idealistic criteria to assess the selection work of some trained, some semi-trained and some mostly untrained workers. Notions about personality, emotional maturity, motivation and quality of relationships are open to several interpretations, as they have no clear definition and no defined boundaries. To the untrained and uninitiated, these notions must spell even greater uncertainty and anxiety.

To limit the task to manageable numbers, five cases from each agency were carefully studied, the information classified under each topic and item and subsequently graded. All the selection information available on each case was classified under one of the nine topics outlined above. To minimise the element of subjectivity each topic was further sub-divided into items, also deduced from social work theory. The total number of items reached was 40. The detailed analysis of the 60 cases (which appears in the main study), showed the extent to which the material in each case covered the topics and items suggested by the profession. Our task was made easier by the very scanty information available on which such vital decisions were made. In some instances this did not go beyond factual identifying information.

Number of interviews with each couple: There are no set rules about the number of times a couple ought to be seen before the study is completed. Rowe [33] suggests at least four. To reach an understanding of the complex psychological and emotional factors involved, it is thought that a series of interviews are necessary. The formulated practice of at least one agency in the sample, was to hold an interview in the office with the couple together, an interview with the wife on her own – usually combined with a home visit – and one with the husband by himself. A joint interview of husband and wife could sometimes follow before the final assessment was reached.

Five of the twelve agencies in the sample, held only one selection interview, another five held mostly two and the remaining two agencies held three or more. Three of the five agencies, that mainly held one interview, had the poorest ratio of staff to cases but the remaining two had a very favourable one. Though the number of staff and the amount of other resources available appeared to influence practice, this was not always the case. Where practice had become routinised, improvement of the staff to cases ratio did not seem to have much effect, if it was not accompanied by other measures aimed at changing agency policies and programmes.

General findings from the evaluation of the selection material.

One in every three agencies (table 18) failed to assess five or more topics. Only two agencies considered all possible nine topics. The best covered topics were housing and socioeconomic situation. None of the remaining topics was on average covered beyond 30.0% of the "standards" level set by the profession. The most poorly covered topics were, "the

Table 18. Percentage coverage of recommended topics.
(This table was summarised from a detailed analysis which appears in the main study.)

	Topic (i)	Topic (ii)	Topic (iii)	Topic (iv)	Topic (v)	Topic (vi)	Topic (vii)	Topic (viii)	Topic (ix)
Borough I	28	15	24	20	-	12	25	90	60
Borough II	12	-	-	-	-	-	-	85	50
County E	32	15	40	55	48	37	8	85	50
Borough H	-	-	-	10	-	-	-	85	50
County H	24	20	-	35	-	14	20	95	65
County S	57	25	48	45	52	40	40	100	75
Borough W	-	-	-	20	-	-	15	85	50
County W	-	-	-	15	-	-	10	75	55
Independent	60	70	60	60	72	72	80	95	75
Moral	12	15	-	15	32	20	35	70	60
National	37	25	-	40	-	-	20	85	55
Social	28	-	-	25	37	17	25	75	55
Average N	24.2	15.4	14.3	28.3	20.1	17.7	22.8	85.4	60.4

quality of the marital relationship", "emotional maturity" and "attitude toward illegitimacy and unmarried parents". In a final analysis, only ten of the 60 couples were selected on the basis of fifty per cent or more of material suggested by social work literature. The procedure followed for the selection of these ten couples was a very detailed and careful one. At least two agencies, in the sample (County S and Independent) appeared to have given considerable thought to their study process and the characteristics to be looked for. In their selection process these two agencies covered all topics from a fair to considerable extent. However the process in respect of certain topics was structured to such a point that the individual profiles did not fully emerge. The selection methods used by all 12 agencies were mostly a combination of the interviewing and administrative approach but at least five of them predominantly used the administrative method.

The selection of the 60 couples was, with some notable exceptions, mainly decided on the basis of factual and environmental information rather than on an assessment of their personality and attitudes. Possession of a comfortable home, a steady occupation and good income, appeared to be the decisive factors. Ten of the agencies had no organised approach to their selection work and the assessment of many couples often reflected the views and sometimes the value judgments of individual workers. Statements like "these are respectable people and should be allowed to adopt", or "these are very nice and sensible people", or "very nice, very happy couple", was the only personal information about many applicants. Such assessments could not be deduced from the factual nature of the rest of the material. It was assumed that, because adoption workers in voluntary societies had to submit their reports to case-committees, they would be motivated to prepare informative ones but this was so only in a minority of cases. The conclusion from these findings is that vital decisions about the selection of couples were reached on the basis of a very limited range of factors and that case-committees, where they existed, acted mainly as rubber-stamps for their own or for their caseworkers' recommendations. The expertise often claimed for agency selections was justified by performance only in a minority of cases.

A serious gap was found to exist between actual practice and social work expectations, as well as between professed and actual practice. Only exceptionally, theory and findings from research appeared to percolate down the agency structure and influence practice in some form. Currently a lot of theory appears to transcend national boundaries very rapidly, especially from the more "developed" areas with full complements of trained staff, to other areas where this form of work has not received equivalent attention. On these occasions there is a real danger in thinking that, once theory is put to paper, it is also practised. In a less "developed" area, such theories are often super-imposed on the work of untrained staff who do not have the necessary background to absorb them and relate them to what they are doing.

Conclusions

From 1960 through 1965 there was a slight drop in the
number of applicants per child. This was mainly due to a
sudden increase in the number of illegitimate children born
and subsequently of those released for adoption. Almost
three quarters of those who originally applied to the agencies
were approved, over ten per cent were rejected and fifteen per
cent withdrew. Agencies were found to be using a variety of
eligibility criteria, mostly based on assumptions about their
relevance for 'good' adjustment. These criteria were applied
with more or less rigidity depending on the particular agency's
orientation and the margin between the number of applicants
and the number of babies available. Though there has been
some shift away from certain rigid criteria, it would still
be difficult for applicants who were not christians, had not
been married for more than three years, where the wife was
over 40 or who were re-married, to adopt a young, healthy
infant of Caucasian extraction. In certain areas of the
country it is even more difficult if the applicants belong to
social classes IV and V.

The selection of adoptive couples was mainly decided on
the basis of factual and environmental information and only
exceptionally on an assessment of the emotional, personal
and psychological suitability of the applicants. To a large
extent, however, whether a couple are accepted as adoptive
parents, depends on what type of child they want and to which
agency they apply. The latter, of course, may be determined
by the area in which a couple happen to live. In certain
instances there was indication that the principle of 'less
eligibility' was applied in the selection of certain applicants. Only one agency had formulated its methods to reflect
some organised approach to the selection of adoptive couples.

CHAPTER NINE

THE 'MATCHING' PROCESS

Theories in child development have stressed the importance of stable family relationships as a factor in healthy
child development. The effect of these theories on adoption
was the strengthening of the belief that the success of the adoption situation was very much dependent on the integration of
the child into the family. Because of this, a conviction developed among adoption caseworkers that a reasonable matching
of parents and child, in as many attributes as possible, was
likely to reduce friction and lead to success. Every effort
was, therefore, made to place a child with as far as possible
similar characteristics to those of the adoptive parents.
The practice of matching parents and child came to be associated with a stress on similarity in such aspects as physical
appearance, personality, temperament, intellectual capacity,
race, cultural background, religion etc.

Though the word 'matching' was used extensively, especially in the forties and fifties, agencies never really
spelled-out what this amounted to. Some agencies in the
United States were proud to advertise their matching practices as an attraction to adopters and as a means of deterring
independent arrangements. The Louisiana department of Public
Health, for instance, in a brochure published in 1950, said
about its adoption matching practices: "A licensed agency
places a child in your home who is as far as possible like the
child who might have been born to you and who is likely to
grow into the kind of person who can share your family's interests and be looked on as your child. Licensed agencies generally try to find a child whose physical characteristics,
mental capacities, personality, nationality and religious background are comparable to those of the adoptive family". The
Oklahoma State Department of Social Welfare claimed to be able
to tell adopters about the child's heritage, his physical and
mental development, his emotional stability and above all
about his potentialities, all attributes that would be as near
their own as possible. The concept of 'matching' was copied
by many agencies in Britain as an ideal objective to strive
for.

Steinman, [52] writing as far back as 1953, warned that
there was a great deal of fear among adoption workers of even
considering that perhaps there are children and families who
can accept a great deal in the way of differences. He criticised the lack of help to prospective adopters to develop
their capacities for the acceptance of difference. In the
same year, Davis and Bouck [53] wrote that matching in physical
appearance, racial background and intellectual potential did
not have the weight often given it by the workers, by many of
the applicants and by the lay public. Similarly Loeb[54] in
1956 was saying that "there is ... more mystery and less fact
in the matching process than elsewhere in adoption practice".

The practice of trying to match parents and child appeared to be based mostly on assumptions rather than on proven facts. As such, it went through various stages over the last twenty to thirty years. For example, in the forties and fifties, many agencies - mainly in the States - considered cultural background as an absolute necessity, likewise nationality and skin-colour. Ten years later, they were described as of little importance. Gradually, it was beginning to dawn on many adoption workers in the field that what were often community prejudices were being projected as matching necessities. The Child Welfare League's standards manual, [37] though implying that "similarities of background or characteristics should not be a major consideration in the selection of a family", added "except when integration of the child into the family and his identification with them may be facilitated by likeness, as in the case of some older children or some children with distinctive physical traits such as skin-colour". In the 4th edition of the "standards manual" in 1965, the League changed its position considerably and simply recommended that "similarities of background or characteristics should not be a major consideration in the selection of a family". The emphasis now was on the ability of adoptive parents to accept the child as he is or may develop, regardless of how he may differ from them. It rightly pointed out that people vary in their capacity to accept difference. It was Kirk [50] who finally provided evidence to support the view that "acknowledgement of difference" by the adopters was conducive "to good communication and to order and dynamic stability in adoptive families." He also claimed that rejection of difference was conducive "to poor communications with subsequent disruptive results for the adoptive relationship". The adoption workers' attempt to produce, through adoption, the natural looking family, does not make it easy for adopters to acknowledge the difference. On this point, Rowe, [33] though supporting the general view that difference must be accepted, stresses that difference should not be accentuated or sought for its own sake. In our postal questionnaire, agencies were asked to say which of ten factors they use when trying to match child and adoptive parents. Their answers are listed (table 19) in order of importance, but it is recognised that one should be cautious in drawing too many conclusions from them. Though the majority of agencies claimed to use almost all ten factors listed, as a basis for matching, it is obvious that individual circumstances would greatly determine the extent of their occurrence. Some of the matching aspects that agencies claimed to carry out would be impossible, because of the lack of appropriate resources and professional expertise. What agencies possibly mean is that they make an effort to match parents and children on these characteristics, by using their personal judgment.

From a study of the case records, the only evidence of matching found was that based on concrete, or what appeared to be apparent characteristics. There was a general attempt to match socio-economic background, religion, race and, to a

Table 19. The Basis for Matching

Matching factors considered important	Total Number of responses	Yes	No
(a) Level of intelligence and intellectual potential	42	39	3
(b) Religious background	42	39	3
(c) Physical resemblance to child	42	33	9
(d) Cultural background	40	30	10
(e) Physical characteristics of child's family	41	28	13
(f) Geographic separation from parents	39	27	12
(g) Racial background	42	22	20
(h) Temperamental needs	42	22	20
(i) Educational background	42	21	21
(j) Nationality background	40	16	24

lesser extent, physical resemblance. Agencies also believed that matching by socio-economic background eventually brought about intellectual matching too. Some matching practices we came across appeared not only to encourage a "rejection of difference" but were likely to reinforce dysfunction in children and adopters. There was little evidence to show that such matching was arranged in response to the adopters' wishes, and it appeared to represent the agencies' belief in what constitutes good future adjustment.

Intellectual and social matching: As 95 per cent of the children placed with non-relatives, were less than a year old at the time of placing, their intellectual assessment would have been almost impossible. Intelligence tests for infants have in the last decade or so been discredited, because of their low predictive value. It is now widely accepted that there is no satisfactory evidence that tests given to babies before the age of 18 months to three years will predict later intelligence. Wittenborn's[44] study of adoptive children concluded that prediction was a somewhat fruitless activity and the efforts devoted to assessing the infant could be better used in studying the adoptive applicants. Some agencies here assume, however, that a child of superior parents is more likely to be superior than a child of dull parents. These agencies used as a guide to intelligence the natural parents occupation and sometimes the parents' education. One agency used to administer intelligence tests to biological mothers and when feasible to biological fathers as an aid to the matching processes. No such tests were administered to adoptive applicants. Studies on the subject of intellectual matching have helped to dispel a number of misconceptions, though the final verdict may still be open. Skodak and Skeels [55] in an extensive study of children with inferior histories placed with adoptive parents, found that children adopted into homes of higher socio-economic status than those into which they were born, tended to develop intellectual ability commensurate with their adoptive homes. The findings appear to highlight the importance that environment must play in determining a child's eventual intellectual attainment, though it is acknowledged that it cannot create ability that is not there. The studies by Wittenborn [44] and Witmer [40] supported Skodak and Skeels findings. Humphrey and Ounsted [56] also confirmed that the children's ability and achievement tended to be closely related to the adoptive parents' status. The question posed is how far agencies by continuing to stress intellectual matching, foster greater expectations in adopters, who later come to feel cheated, if expectations are not met by the child.

Some of the evidence we came across suggested that some adoption workers make assumptions about the kind of child the family would like. Such comments by workers as "only a child of superior parents would do for this couple", or "only a child from a good middle-class background will do", were not infrequent. In one instance a case committee was considering turning down the placement of a clerkess's child with a couple, where the man was a university lecturer, on the ground that the child's intellectual potential would not match up with that of the adopters. At the next meeting of the case committee, the caseworker in charge of the case, produced evidence to show that the biological mother's grand-mother was a graduate, and so "good achievement could be expected from the child". On hearing this, the committee approved the placement. The fact, that the child had to wait in foster-care for another three weeks before it was finally placed, could itself have adverse effects on its subsequent adjustment within the adoptive family. Social work literature stresses that "the educational achievement of the child's own family, whether limited or advanced, should not influence the selection of a family".[37]

The attitude towards this type of matching was further illustrated by two agencies who said that in their adoption work the only difficulty was in finding adopters for "working class children," but at the same time they had plenty of middle-class applicants. Similarly, the secretary of one adoption society is reported to have told 'The People' (11.5.69):

"We are finding that babies from a middle-class background, which we usually place with good-class adoptive families, are not available in such numbers as before .... In our society we take great pains to match the baby precisely with the adopting parents, and it is getting increasingly difficult". That social class background should become a decisive factor in adoption placings appears to be contrary to the professed principles of social work philosophy. Apart from these considerations, this kind of commitment makes agency practice appear adoptive parent, rather than child, orientated. Witmer et al [40] found from their extensive study, that the adoption outcome was not influenced by the socio-economic characteristics of the adopting family, provided the home was economically stable. Ripple [51] found no association between matching appearance and background with favourable outcome.

In the general matching process, it was also usual for some agencies to try and match similarities in interests or studies. For instance the child of a student of music was placed with the family of a director of music; that of a mathsstudent with a quantity surveyor, the child of a nurse was placed with a medical practioner, that of shop-assistant with a packer; the child of a waitress with a factory worker, that of a clerkess with a Bank teller and so on. Children in general were adopted in homes of a higher socio-economic background than that of their natural mothers. Though it is possible that some stress may be created by placing children, who are poorly endowed, with couples who are themselves too socially and intellectually orientated, the appropriate practical measure to avoid this would be to focus attention at the selection stage on identifying such extreme attitudes and assessing how rigid they are.

Religious Background: The Adoption Act gives the right to the natural parent to specify the religion in which he would like the child to be brought up. The agency, therefore, has an obligation to match the wishes of the parents with the religious persuation of the adopters. The law, however, is entirely neutral about the adopters' religion, when the biological parent gives an unconditional consent. Of the number of adoption orders granted to non-relatives in 1965, the natural parents specified a religion in three out of every five cases. Though religion appears to be a straight forward matching operation, a pattern emerged from the practices of the twelve agencies which suggested that the adoption worker's own preferance might be invoked during the process. For instance, for children surrendered through some agencies (not necessarily denominational) there was a hundred per cent preference expressed, whilst for children adopted through some other agencies, there was a hundred per cent no preference. Such patterns occasionally changed when there was a change of caseworker. In other words, in some agencies workers insisted that the mothers always specified a religious preference, in others, they did not appear to draw the mother's attention to it. This was perhaps out of fear that a preference might lead to difficulties in finding adopters who could match with such a preference.

Temperamental needs: Though most of the agencies answering our postal questionnaire said that they try to match the child's temperamental needs to those of the adopters, no evidence was found from the records to support this claim. Matching by temperament is obviously important when placing older children, but as 95 per cent of the children were placed when under a year old, it is doubtful how practicable this would have been for these infants. Only in a minority of cases agencies had sufficient information about the infants they placed to lead to any recognition of temperamental needs such as irritability, activity, response, eating and sleeping habits and hence to evaluate them for matching purposes.

Racial background: It is recognised that racial characteristics, being genetic in origin, and not subject to change, cannot be sidestepped in adoption. However irrational colour preference may be, the placement agency needs to satisfy itself that no child will be placed in a home where it is likely to suffer because of this. Agencies that use racial background as a basis for matching, may be doing it either because they believe that non-white children are of inferior stock, or because they want to protect the child from problems likely to be created by the social environment within which it is going to find itself.

Cultural and Nationality background: Three out of every four agencies say that they try to match the child's cultural background with that of the adopters, and two out of five that they try to match children and parents by nationality background. Nationality and culture are not inherent in human beings but are acquired depending on the group within which the individual has been reared. Jehu [57] also stresses that personality and behavioural differences between racial or national groups are due to cultural and historical influences. In matching, therefore, we may dismiss cultural and nationality differences as of little or no importance, though cultural differences can be important when placing older children. In spite of what agencies claimed, in practice they placed children of Irish mothers with Scottish and English families; children of Canadian, Australian and Dutch parentage were adopted by Scottish and English families and Scottish children were adopted by American families. Perhaps, when we talk of different culture and nationality we are really referring to people with negroid or dark features, in which case it is the colour of the child's skin that appears to highlight his different cultural background.

Physical resemblance: Four out of every five agencies said that they use physical resemblance as a basis for matching. Apart from the great difficulty in matching the physical characteristics of very young babies, the practice appears to meet the agency's need for a tangible form of matching, rather than its being a response to adopters' requirements. Kreech in discussing Ripple's [51] findings laments the fact that in spite of the findings and experience in the field, there are still those who insist that similarity in appearance is conducive to identification and, therefore, of great importance.

Conclusion:

The current view appears to be that the emphasis should shift from stressing similarities, in the adoptive situation, to helping adopters to recognise inherent difference, without necessarily aiming at differences for their own sake. Our findings suggest that adoption practice does not appear to have been significantly influenced by some of the findings of studies in child development which stress the beneficial effects of an enabling environment on the development of the personality. A biologistic determinism was identified in the practices of most agencies. The practice at the moment is to place the children with the most favourable background history in the home with the best 'apparent' potential, and to place the children with the poorest history in homes with the less obvious potential.

CHAPTER   TEN

POST-PLACEMENT SUPERVISION

Between placement and legal adoption, a responsibility is
laid on the adoption agency and the local authority to pay what
have come to be known as "supervisory" visits. The adoption
agency's responsibility stops when the prospective adopters
notify the local authority of their intention to adopt. It
then becomes the responsibility of the local authority to
arrange for the family to be visited by a child care officer until the order is granted, or until the child attains the age of
eighteen. In the case of independent placments, the whole responsibility for supervisory visits rests with the local authority. No such supervision is required in cases where one of the
applicants to the adoption is a parent. In all other circumstances, no order can be granted unless the family has been
under this form of supervision for at least three months. In
actual fact, adoption societies continued in most cases to
supervise their placements even after the adopters had notified
the local authority of their intention to adopt. This meant
that some families were receiving visits both from the adoption
worker, who made the original placing, and also from the local
authority.

Post-placement visits by the placing agency: Social work literature stresses the importance of early visits to help the
adopters with possible initial difficulties of integration, or
with other anxieties arising from the adoption situation. It
is claimed that the worker, who has known the family before
placement, is also in the best position to help in the post-
placement period. The regulations provide that each agency
must arrange that every infant is visited within one month
after being placed, and that, after each visit, the caseworker
visiting should make a report to the case committee "as to the
welfare of the infant".

Five of the 12 agencies in the sample, usually visited
the child and the adopters within the first fortnight after
placement. Another five visited between four and six weeks
after placement, but one of these paid no visits to at least
one third of its placements. The remaining two agencies did
not indicate in their records whether any visits had been
paid at all. None of the agencies appeared to submit a
written report to their case committees. The average number
of visits paid between placement and legal adoption was two.
The farther the placement was from the agency's base the
fewer were the visits. The number of visits did not appear
to be determined by the individual needs of the families or
children but rather reflected the practices of the agency concerned. No increased visits were paid, for instance, in
cases where the selection study had shown areas of possible
difficulties.

Apart from the two agencies that had no records of any

post-placement visits, the remaining ten, with one exception, kept very little information mainly noting that a visit had been paid and that the child appeared well-looked after. Only in exceptional cases was some reference made to the impact of the child's presence on the family. There was no suggestion from the records that the adoption worker involved herself in any problem-solving' activity with the adopters, or that significant anxieties were shared. Difficulties were revealed only in three instances. In one of these the adoptive father had had lengthy psychiatric treatment and though the family doctor did not recommend him to the agency, the consultant psychiatrist, who was treating him, maintained that the adoptive father's condition would not affect the adoption situation. Soon after the placement of the child, the couple started raising considerable doubts about the child's future potential and about the quality of his background. The visiting worker remarked, after one of her visits: "I rather felt that a baby from a better sort of background might have been placed here". Subsequently she promised the couple a 'superior' child for their second adoption.

Adoption workers in general focussed their visits on the child's health rather than on his interaction with the family. This may have discouraged adopters from raising wider issues. Certainly little evidence was found to support the view that adoptive parents will want to talk about such topics as their inability to have children, anxieties about heredity and illegitimacy, doubts about their capacity for parenthood and so on. Neither were any difficulties with the child shared. It is very possible that adopters do not feel secure enough at this stage to share difficulties or anxieties with a visitor who still has the power to remove the child or at least to refuse the placement of a further one. The question could also be raised of how far the visiting workers showed by their attitude and handling of situations that they were able and prepared to listen and help.

Statutory supervision: The purpose of statutory supervision is undefined and vague. No clarified objectives and procedures have been worked out, neither has any consideration been given as to whether supervision is really helpful and for whom. The law assumes that it is necessary to secure the well-being of the child, but its effectiveness has not been tested. Social work theory has given only scanty attention to this important matter and has not, in effect, helped to identify the practical implications of the provisions, nor the conflicts within the supervisor's role. No one appears to have spelled-out whether they are merely official observers or whether they should use the opportunity of visiting for problem-solving. Their lack of understanding of their function must make it difficult for them to explain it to the adoptive couples, and the latter must feel equally confused about the supervisor's presence, especially when the adoption worker is still visiting. No evidence was found to suggest

that supervisors made significant efforts to clarify for the
adopters the purpose of the visits and how they could be used.
This possibly contributed to the fact that none of the adopters
used the opportunity of contact as one for discussion of doubts,
difficulties or anxieties. The supervisors themselves used the
few visits they paid as an opportunity to observe tangible conditions, rather than to help in the resolution or discussion of
possible difficulties. No supervisor attempted a plan or out-
line to guide him in working with the adoptive family during
the probationary period. Two other factors contributed to
make the value of supervision doubtful: the lack of co-
operation between the placing and supervising agency (except
where the same authority also placed the child) and that between the supervising agency and the court. An absolute dich-
otomy appeared to exist between the work of the placing agency
and that of the supervising authority. Though the placing
agency had at its disposal significant information about the
adopters and the child, none of this was shared with the supervising authority. No social reports, for instance, accompanied the notification, to the local authority, and no effort
was made to make the local authority aware of any particular
circumstances or difficulties that might arise and with which
the adopters might need help. The failure also of most courts
to ask the supervising authority for a report, did not stimulate interest on the part of the supervising worker who eventually came to see this task as one peripheral to his main
activities.

The average number of supervisory visits paid to each
case during the average six month probationary period was
1.6, but one in every ten cases was not visited at all, and
only 3.3% of the cases received three or more visits. The
majority of families were visited twice, but this included,
in most cases, one visit that customarily is paid for the
preparation of the curator's report. Two authorities did not
arrange for any supervisory visits to be paid at all, whilst
two others delegated this responsibility to the district
nurse. The district nurse became yet another person to be
added to the multiplicity of persons and agencies involved
in the adoption situation. Among the cases supervised by
local authorities, there were 33 where the children had been
placed either by a third party or directly by the mother.
There was no difference in the number or content of visits
paid to these children and families, compared with agency
placements. The supervisors did not depart from stereotyped
visits to give more time and to pay extra attention to this
type of adoption. The total pattern that emerged was one
of visits being paid in a routine way, because of the statutory responsibility, rather than being dictated by the
needs of each case. It was characteristic of the superficial
nature of these visits that in a number of supervisions involving adoption by grand-parents, the supervisors did not
come to know that some of the older children were ignorant of
the fact that they were not the natural children of their
grand-parents. This important fact was later revealed to the

Court.

A careful analysis of case-records showed that the visits were mostly child-focussed, with little or no reference to the adopters. The supervisors saw themselves mainly as observers, rather than as catalysts for possible difficulties. The focus mainly on the child's health negates the possibility that the adopters may have doubts, fears or anxieties which they may want to talk about. It is difficult to say how far the adopters' reluctance to share problems with the supervisor was because the latter represented a threat to them or whether it was because of the supervisor's failure to plan and visit more frequently. Planned visits could have helped to establish a relationship that would have encouraged discussion and sharing. Because this is a period when the adopters are chiefly anxious to see the adoption through, it may, however, be too much to expect them to share doubts and difficulties with an authority figure, who could prevent them from achieving the long-cherished aim of becoming parents.

Conclusion

There is an urgent need to re-examine the whole concept of adoption supervision, to clarify its objectives and review its appropriateness. Its value as an instrument of public control is very doubtful whilst its existence simply helps to perpetuate an unjustified sense of adequacy. Practice has hitherto failed to demonstrate the usefulness of supervision as a method contributing to the integration of the child into the adoptive family.

CHAPTER ELEVEN

THE PRACTICE OF THE COURTS

Adoption orders in Scotland may be granted by three different courts: (i) the High Court, (ii) the Sheriff Court, and (iii) the Juvenile Court. In 1965 only four orders were granted by the High Court and none by the Juvenile Courts. The tradition of submitting petitions to the latter type of court had not developed. This leaves the Sheriff Court as the main one handling adoption applications. The function of the Sheriff Court in matters of adoption is laid down in the 1958 Adoption Act and in the Act of Sederunt (Adoption of Children regulations), 1959. Amendments to the regulations were introduced in January, 1967 after the commencement of this study. Because of this, a second visit was paid to some of the courts in the autumn of 1968.

The Sheriff Court has extensive jurisdiction in both civil and criminal cases, and the Sheriff, who presides over it, is a legally qualified professional judge. The court process in adoption usually starts with a request by the adoption agency for a serial number to be allocated to the prospective adopters. This number will subsequently appear on the consent form which the natural parent is asked to sign. The regulations make suitable provision for preventing the disclosure of the adopters' identity to the natural parent of the child. There is no similar provision to protect the mother's identity from the adopters. This can depend on the practice of the agency or of the solicitor handling the petition forms. The Act provides that the mother's surrender of the child is to the adopters and not the agency. This provision often causes the agencies some anxiety, because some natural mothers are likely to disappear before suitable adopters have been found. A request to the court for a serial number may also come retrospectively if the child was originally placed on a fostering basis until it reached the age of six weeks. It is not unusual, however, for the agencies to ask the court for a serial number and later on to cancel it. From the registers of the surveyed courts it was found that the number of cancellations amounted to 2.6 per cent of agency placements, but the majority of these 'breakdowns' occurred to the placements of two agencies, which suggested some undue hurry in the process. A cancellation of a serial number may happen (a) if the natural mother changes her mind before she signs her consent; (b) if the adopters change their mind before they lodge a petition and decide to return the child; and (c) when the agency itself decides to remove the child, provided again that no petition has been lodged with the court. Once an applicantion is lodged no child can be removed except with the approval of the court.

Prospective adopters petition the court by completing a set form which asks for a fair amount of factual information. To avoid revealing to the adopters the name and address of the natural parent(s), the petition is usually, but not always,

handled and completed by the placing agency or its solicitor
and later placed with the court. In the case of third party
placements, this is usually done by the third party or the
solicitor acting for the family which means that the mother's
name and address may more easily be revealed to the adopters.
In agency placements, the completion and retention of the
application by the agency, gives the latter considerable control over the timing of its lodgement. This can increase the
petitioners' dependence on the agency, especially if the
latter feels that it knows best when the application should be
lodged. The legal provision is that an application can be
lodged at any time following the child's placement, provided
that the infant is at least six weeks old. No court order,
however, can be made unless the welfare authority has been
supervising the placement for at least three months. Though
it is possible for an adoption order to be made at the end of
three months following the placement, the average period
found by the study was six and a half months (excluding those
cases where there were good reasons for long delays). One
main reason for the delays was that in 90% of the cases,
agencies waited unnecessarily for approximately three months,
following the child's placement, before lodging the petition.

THE CURATOR AD LITEM

The function and role of the curator ad litem has been
outlined in the successive Adoption Acts and Regulations from
1930 onwards. Specific areas of enquiries are outlined under
the Scottish Act of Sederunt (Adoption of Children) 1959 and
1967. The curator ad litem is an official acting for the
court and his main responsibility is to safeguard the interests of the child before the court and to satisfy the latter
that an adoption order, if made, will be for the welfare of
the child. For this reason he is expected to carry out "a full
expert investigation on behalf of the court before an adoption
order is made". He is expected to confirm certain facts,
interview the various parties involved, assess relationships
and express an opinion about the petitioners' personality and
suitability to adopt. The purpose of the curator's report is
to place the court in a better position to decide the child's
ultimate future. This report forms almost the only basis on
which the decision is made and for a number of reasons outlined below, some of which are peculiar to Scotland, this report assumes great importance in influencing the outcome of
the adoption petition:

(i) The curator is the only representative of the court who
has an opportunity to interview all parties and assess the
situation. Unlike England, the Scottish Act of Sederunt
(Adoption of Children) 1959, leaves it to the discretion of
the court whether to fix a hearing or not. It was only exceptionally that Sheriffs did so. The absence of a hearing
deprives the court of a first-hand view of the applicants to
enable it to exercise its own judgement, in addition to con-

sidering the views and recommendations contained in the curator's report.

(ii)   The curator is not present when the Sheriff considers the application. Decisions are taken by him in the privacy of his Chambers at a time of his own choosing. This system deprives the curator of an opportunity to give additional verbal explanation, if required. It further deprives him of the opportunity to understand the kind of report and information that the Sheriff finds helpful in reaching his decision.

(iii)   By the time the curator is appointed, there have been at least two other 'official' persons in the picture: the placing agency's worker who often carries on supervision until the order is granted and the local authority supervising officer, who is fulfilling a statutory obligation. In chapter ten it was pointed out that there was virtually no co-operation and co-ordination between the adoption agency and the supervising agency, and that each worker was acting in isolation and to the exclusion of the other. In Chapters 7 and 8 it was also found that the work of some placing agencies was hasty and superficial. Both the adoption agency and the supervising agency appear to assume that the curator is a safeguard for their practices and, because of this, the onus is finally placed on him to carry out his responsibilities thoroughly, if the welfare of the child is to be ensured.

    The idea of a completely independent investigation is basic to the present role of the curator. He is not expected to repeat work already done, or work that should have been done with natural and adoptive parents, or to offer counselling. His job is to ascertain the facts, assess the whole situation and give his opinion about the placement to the court. If the obligation was simply to ascertain the facts, then this could have been a less controversial role and one that could easily be fulfilled by any court clerk, who could go over the application papers and make sure that they were in order. However, the regulations, as well as the Home Office publications, see this role as going well beyond an ascertainment of facts. The question that arises, therefore, is what kind of person would be most suitably equipped to carry out this function effectively. The Hurst committee said that only a trained social worker could be expected to make valid assessment of the all-important emotional factors, such as the relationship between the adopters and the child, and their reasons for wishing to adopt him.[17] Those who support this view add that solicitors, who are still being appointed as curators by some Scottish courts, are qualified neither by training nor by experience to carry out this important function. The Home Office recommends that the children's officer, or a member of his staff, be asked to serve as curator in all adoption cases, except those in which the child concerned has been placed by the same children's officer. In contrast to this view, there

is also the view put to us by some courts that the ability to
evaluate personality and human relationships arises out of a
common sense approach. These courts stressed mainly the legal
and factual side of the curator's work. Courts, that took this
line mainly (but not always) appointed solicitors to act as
curators. Some of the courts, however, who saw the role of the
curator as involving certain skills compatible with social work,
tried to appoint social workers but were occasionally prevented
from doing so, either because the children's department was too
busy and understaffed, or because this department failed to put
its work across to the courts. More recently, because of the
failure of some of the new social work departments to provide
curators' reports within a reasonable time, a number of courts
that were previously appointing social workers as curators,
have reverted to the old system of appointing solicitors. This
was seen by adoption workers as a necessary but rather retro-
grade step. There are fears that this may be an indication of
how little priority the new departments may accord to this
type of work.

The Evaluation of the Curators' Reports

In summary, the role of the curator ad litem is to ascertain certain facts and to assess the placement in the context
of personal relationships. To do this, he will need to interview all the parties involved and observe behaviour and interaction, where appropriate. The two aspects of his work usually
go together but, for purposes of evaluation we decided to concentrate on the second aspect of his function. Factual aspects,
such as names, dates, addresses and so on were usually well
checked. Our task was to classify and evaluate the less tangible
aspects of the curator's work. The intangibles were elicited
from the provisions of the regulations and from official reports on the matter. These were grouped under the following
5 topics: Information and assessments about:

(i)   the natural parents, the circumstances of the child's
        surrender and the signing of the consents;

(ii)   observations about the child and its development;

(iii)   observations on the adoptive couple and, where
        appropriate, on their other children and the
        general interaction and atmosphere within the
        family;

(iv)   consultation with the supervising authority; and

(v)   a final assessment of the situation followed by
        the appropriate recommendation.

To minimise the element of subjectivity in the process of
classifying the material, the five topics were sub-divided
into nine relevant items and information was grouped under
each item.

The 1030 reports which reached the courts, were prepared

by 60 curators. For purposes of evaluation it was decided to
study three reports submitted by each curator. The decision to
evaluate only three reports was based on the observation during
the pilot study, that there was virtually no difference between
different reports submitted by the same curator. Because of
the argument as to whether the curator should be a social
worker or a solicitor, the 180 reports were classified by the
type of curator. The final situation was:

(a)	Trained social workers	9	Reports evaluated	27
(b)	Untrained social workers	26	Reports evaluated	78
(c)	Solicitors	25	Reports evaluated	75
	TOTAL	60		180

Summary findings: Table 20 summarises, by topic and type of
curator, all detailed tables, analysing and rating the content
of the 180 reports submitted by the 60 curators to the 20
courts. (The detailed analysis appears in the main study).
This table shows that no individual topic was covered ade-
quately in more than 34.0 per cent of cases. The best covered
topic (34.0%) was the one referring to the natural parents.
The topics least covered were the ones referring to the adopters and to the child. The general conclusion from this table
was that curators were efficient in checking concrete facts but
only exceptionally did they attempt assessments of persons or
situations. In spite of the importance that the law attaches
to these investigations, the curators themselves appeared to
lack conviction about their value. Only a minority saw their
role as including observations and assessments of the psycho-
social circumstances of the parties involved. Vital contacts
with the supervising agency were not always established, whilst
the placing agency was only exceptionally contacted. Assessments were attempted only in a minority of cases and this
appeared to reflect the curators' lack of certainty about
their focus and the absence of a relevant body of knowledge
that would have helped them to arrive at such assessments.
None of the 1030 reports contained any reservations on any
applicants personal suitability to adopt. Investigations and
reports concerning third party and direct placements received
no different or special attention and their serious implications had not been recognised. In a few instances the curators were unaware of this important aspect. Social workers'
reports were only slightly more informative than solicitors,
but the latter generally failed to establish certain vital
contacts. They appeared to be office bound and to lack the
sort of facilities usually associated with a social agency.
Their reports reflected a legalistic approach of ensuring
that the facts were correct, but their other observations,

Table 20. Content of Curators' Reports (Summary Table)
(N.180) (Percentage summaries based on number of reports)

Type of curator	TOPIC NO. 1			TOPIC NO. 2			TOPIC NO. 3			TOPIC NO.4				TOPIC NO. 5	
	No observations	Factual and repetitive	Fair to considerable information	No observations	Factual and repetitive	Fair to considerable information	No assessment	Factual and repetitive	Fair to considerable information	No consultation	Verbal contact	Written report	No assessment	Factual and repetitive	Fair to considerable information
S/Worker (Trained)	8	43	49	46	26	28	65	11	24	39	28	33	16	52	32
S/Workers (Untrained)	11	37	52	53	22	25	59	18	23	36	26	38	8	54	38
Solicitors	12	76	12	40	36	24	61	18	21	53	36	11	12	65	23
% Average	11	55	34	47	28	25	61	16	23	43	31	26	11	58	31
(N)	20	98	62	84	51	45	110	29	41	77	56	47	20	104	56

where, these were included, reflected a lay man's point of view. The latter was also true of many reports submitted by social workers.

The natural parents: The Act offers the parent a last minute opportunity to re-affirm or withdraw his consent to the adoption It is maintained that, depending on the way the curator interviews the parent, he may influence his decision or occasionally create a dilemma about the wisdom of his action. This delicate aspect strengthens the argument of those who would like the curator to be a trained social worker. Curators interviewed personally 28.5 per cent of the natural mothers and another 20.0 per cent were interviewed on their behalf. Solicitors, acting as curators, interviewed personally only 7.0 per cent of the mothers. Curators generally made very little effort to interview putative fathers. The Regulations provide that, if it comes to the notice of the curator that a putative father wishes to be heard by the court on the question whether an adoption order should be made, he is to inform the court so that the latter may consider whether notice of the hearing should be served on him. Of 926 illegitimate children in the sample, the fathers of 34 (or 3.7%) were interviewed by the curators. The 34 fathers had either acknowledged paternity of the child by registering it in their name, or were contributing for its maintenance. Eleven per cent of the reports supplied to the courts, failed to mention the natural parents and only just over a third of the reports contained some individual descriptions about the circumstances of the surrender and the mother's views.

Observations about the child: There was a general failure on the part of most curators to comment about the children's current progress, their adaptation within the family and their interaction with the petitioners or with the petitioners' other children. Older children were rarely interviewed or seen by the curator. Almost 47.0% of the reports gave only the child's name, date of birth and date of placement. The only meaningful observations about the children came from curators whose reports had not been stylised to follow a repetitive form.

Observations on the petitioners and on their other children (where appropriate): It is expected that, as a result of thorough investigations, the curator will be able to advise the court about the applicants' suitability, and about whether the contemplated adoption is "consistent with the welfare of the infant". Three fifths of the reports made no reference to the applicants' personality. No such assessment was attempted and the adopters did not emerge as people from reading the reports. Instead, the reports concentrated mainly on the couple's socio-economic situation. The presence of other children in the family (46.0% of cases) was generally ignored.

Consultation with the supervising authority: Only two of the

20 courts surveyed, made the supervising authority respondent
to the application. The rest of the courts possibly expected
the curator to consult the local authority. In 43.0% of the
cases, however, there was no contact between the curator and
the supervising authority. (Note was taken of those cases
where the supervising worker was also the curator ad litem).
Solicitors failed almost uniformally to consult the supervising
agency, about the placement. Earlier on we noted the failure
of placing agencies to co-operate with supervising agencies
and now a similar failure was found between curators and
supervising officers.

Final assessment of the situation followed by the appropriate
recommendation: An opinion can only be as good as the information on which it is based. This in turn seems to depend on
the investigator's interviewing skills and his ability to
elicit significant information and to observe relevant behaviour, including marital and family interaction. Reports which
simply confirmed facts, ended with a repetitive and stereo-
typed recommendation and with no assessment of the total situation. In other reports, the opinions expressed could not
be deduced from therest of the report. Assessments that at
the outset appeared to be of a more individual nature, lost
their value when it was noted that they were repeated verbatim in subsequent reports and for different placings. Just
under a third of the reports, however, made some attempt to
produce a final assessment, together with an appropriate recommendation. There was more individuality and each report
differed from the others submitted by the same curator. An
obvious effort had been made to study and assess each situation separately and information was supplied that could
help the court arrive at a more discriminating decision.

The classification and rating of the reports by topic
does not tell us much about the whole report, as one report
may cover one or two topics fairly well and simply confirm
the facts for the remaining ones. To get a total picture of
the reports, these were divided into three groups. Reports,
which covered four or five topics from "fair to considerable",
were classified as Informative: reports which covered only
two or three topics from "fair to considerable" were classified as fairly informative; those that covered only one or
less topics from "fair to considerable", were classified as
poor. Three out of every five reports were rated as poor.
The main content of these reports was a rewording of the
factual information contained in the petition and already
known to the court. Only one in every seven reports were rated
as informative and another quarter as fairly informative. The
majority of reports, submitted by all types of curators, were
almost exact copies of previous ones with only factual information to distinguish one from another. Their layout and
content differed only with the agency within which they were
prepared, rather than with the person who prepared them.
Where trained social workers had acted as curators,they too

copied their agencies' pro-forma reports with no effort to de-
viate from routine practices. This, along with the appointment
of trainee social workers to act as curators, reflected the low
status accorded to this type of work within children's departments. Trained and untrained workers, as well as trainees,
copied slavishly forms of reports used by their agency. Workers
when feeling overwhelmed by other responsibilities, tended to
look upon this type of work as a fringe activity to be disposed
of quickly. The impression was formed that, in each social
service department, certain jobs are likely to be delegated as
of lesser importance and consequently may fail to receive more
than minimum attention, and this function seemed to be of such
a nature.

On the basis of these findings the value of the curators'
reports in safeguarding the interests of the children is highly
questionable. Their appointment appears to lead to a sense of
security not justified by the results. The Act obviously
pinned too many expectations and hopes on the extent to which
such investigations could form a safeguard against poor agency
practices. The general conclusion is that the curator's appointment comes too late in the proceedings to be of any practical value to the child. The regulations expect curators to
carry out a kind of function for which many of them are not
trained, nor do they have the necessary body of knowledge
that could enable them to carry out the expert evaluations
and assessments required.

Courts revisited: As a result of the amendments introduced by
the Act of Sederunt (Adoption of Children) 1967, whose objective was to clarify the curator's role, we decided to re-
visit 8 of the 20 courts in the original sample. The aim of
this new study was to establish how far subsequent curators'
reports reflected the new provisions. Our revisit was arranged
eighteen months after the new regulations came into power.
One of the specific points made in the new regulations was
the expectation of curators to provide an assessment of the
petitioner's personality and, "where appropriate that of the
infant, as they are both relevant to the adoption situation".
At our re-visit we analysed and classified 81 reports prepared
by 27 curators. The findings were compared with those found
from the 1965 reports.

Table 21. Courts re-visited: Comparison between
reports submitted in 1965 and 1968

Poor		Fairly Informative		Informative	
1965 %	1968 %	1965 %	1968 %	1965 %	1968 %
59.4	30.0	25.0	39.0	15.6	31.0

Following the introduction of the new rules, there was a

general improvement (table 21) in the content of the curators'
reports. Solicitors' reports fared rather badly in this re-
assessment. A number of social work agencies re-arranged their
reports to incorporate some of the new provisions but none of
the solicitors did so and some reports submitted by other social
work agencies appeared also to have improved, but this was
slightly deceptive as at least three agencies incorporated the
new provisions again in a pro-forma type of reporting. Such
reports conveyed the impression of containing interesting
individual material, but similar material almost in verbatim
form would appear again in subsequent reports submitted by
the same worker, or by another worker from within the same
agency. Some of the improvement noted at one of the courts
appeared to be due to the personal interest of one of the
Sheriffs. It was of interest to note that the curators who
submitted informative reports in 1965, were mainly the ones
who improved their reports even further to reflect the new requirements.

The conclusion reached from these re-visits was that new
legal provisions help to improve practice to some extent.
New provisions, however, appear to be more appropriately used
by agencies already observing good practices. Agencies, that
have been stereotyping their work before, find ways of doing
the same despite any new requirements. It appears, therefore,
that a change of law by itself, without parallel change of
agency practices, can achieve only limited improvements.

Conclusions

In spite of the importance attached to the curators'
investigations, the latter appear to be very uncertain about
the nature of their role and to lack conviction about its importance. Some curators felt that the present form of reporting is 'safe' and avoids possible legal and other complications. Others were generally unaware of the type of information that the courts found useful. An important question
arising out of this is how far the courts encouraged such
routine reports by failing to make different demands. Nat-
urally demands for increased information would put the onus
on the courts for more deliberation on each case. The late
stage in the proceedings at which curators were called in
made them feel impotent in relation to this part of their
work. Two additional and more individual problems seem
also to be involved, indicating personal conflicts for the
curator: (a) Though the curator supplies the court with a
confidential report, it is entirely up to the Sheriff's discretion to decide how to use it in thecase and if and when
there is a hearing. If the report contains only favourable
remarks about either the prospective adopters or the natural
parents there is no trouble. But if the report speaks un-
favourably of either party, its non-disclosure by the court
is likely to be seen as running counter to our notions of
justice. Once adoptions are operated through the courts, the

concept of justice cannot be sidestepped. Disclosure, however, of every report can inhibit the curator and so provide less protection to the child. The report may sometimes have to be based partly on hearsay evidence or confidential information given by the child (if old enough) or by others. Admission of hearsay evidence could be disallowed unless the third parties came to give evidence. The law has failed to make it clear what is the precise status of the confidential report of the curator. (b) The second point is a more personal one for the curator but related to the first. In preparing his report he may feel the conflict between his duty to give the court a full picture of the adoptive applicants and his feelings about the effect on the adopters of an unfavourable report. If he has mixed feelings about the authority vested in him by the court and has not reached some personal conclusions on these issues, he may feel very uncomfortable when faced with the task of formulating assessments and putting his views on paper.

II

THE DECISION OF THE COURT

The Sheriff is the last person in a series of four to make the final decision involving the child's future. Apart from judicial supervision at the moment of making the order, there is no other judicial control over the various stages of the adoption process. The question often asked in connection with the court's adoption work is how far its function is a legal one, a social one or a mixture of both. Blom-Cooper [58] made the point that the process of adoption is not essentially justiciable. He added, "The issues in adoption are hardly susceptible of solution by the application of legal concepts and rules of law". In having to determine whether the order, if made, will be for "the welfare of the child", the court is expected to go beyond the legal into the psycho-social implications too. The Sheriffs, who decide adoption applications, have a legal training but no training in any of the social and behavioural sciences. Similarly, adoption work is only peripheral to the function of the Sheriff court and it rarely receives much attention. A recent committee which reported on the work of the Sheriff Court devoted only seven lines to the court's adoption work, out of a volume of 323 pages. Not only does adoption work appear isolated within the wider function of the Sheriff court, but Sheriffs themselves are isolated from, and unfamiliar with developments in this field. How adoption arrangements eventually work out is still an open question but the Sheriff's isolation from adoption workers, curators and from research findings deprives him of important information and feed-back that could influence his thinking and decision making. The impersonal way in which petitions are now granted does not stimulate curiosity about their eventual outcome. (This should not detract from the fact that a few Sheriffs have shown exceptional interest in adoption matters). If it is agreed that Sheriffs are not qualified by virtue of their training or experience to consider all aspects of adoption, then in their decision-making they are likely to follow either of two procedures: Grant or reject the petition on the basis of whether tangible requirements have been met, or consider both the general requirements and also 'intangibles', aspects regarding the personal suitability of the applicants etc. As the Sheriffs in over 90 per cent of the cases did not see the parties for themselves, they were heavily dependent on the curators reports. Earlier on, however, it was pointed out from the findings that only a minority of curators' reports supplied information on the intangibles. It is recognised that, in situations where the Sheriff is in doubt about the wisdom of granting the order, he will either ask for supplementary investigations or will arrange to see the parties for himself. There was only one instance in which a Sheriff asked the curator for a fresh report because he found the original one very inadequate. Though some Sheriffs were satisfied with the factual reports they were getting, others expressed to us considerable dissatisfaction. It was difficult not to conclude, from the way that well over ninety per cent of the orders were granted, that the courts mainly acted as rubber-stamps for the views of the curators and the placing practices of the adoption agencies. In none of the independent placements, for instance, in which no social agency was involved, did the courts see fit to make the petitioners respondent to the application or to ask for additional information from the curators.

Methods of disposal: When disposing adoption applications, the courts have five possible options: (i) To make a straight-forward adoption order: Such orders are granted on the assumption that they are in the best interests of the child. Of the 1030 applications studied, 1009 were such orders. No conditions were imposed except, where appropriate, a condition about the religion in which the parents wished the child to be brought up. Because of the routine way in which orders were granted, in at least 55 cases the religious requirement was omitted from the order. (ii) To make a provisional order: Fourteen such orders were granted, mainly to U.S.A. service families temporarily stationed here. In none of these cases were background reports obtained from social agencies in the applicants' home countries. (iii) To make an interim order: This provision was not used for any of the cases in the sample. Interim orders can be made in cases where the court is doubtful whether an adoption order should be made. In such cases the local authority is instructed to continue its supervision. The Scottish rules are unclear, however, as to what happens when the interim order expires. In our view, interim orders, could have been appropriate in some cases where the grand-parents wished to adopt their daughter's child but the case was complicated by the fact that the natural mother continued to live with them and relationships were complicated and unclear. There were twenty such cases in the sample. In one case the curator wrote in his report: "I gathered that since returning from the Maternity hospital the mother has informally regarded the child as her sister and her parents as parents of the child. The child regards his mother as his sister and his grand-parents as his parents". The curator then went on to recommend the granting of the order "as the circumstances of the home lead me to consider that the proposed adoption is consistent with the child's welfare". Neither the curator or the court could see the inconsistency between the two comments. Interim orders could also be appropriate in thecase of older children who did not know that they were about to be adopted. Though only seven such cases came to light during the proceedings, an interim order would have given time to the local authority to help the petitioners deal with their feelings about telling the child. Two of the seven children were about to be adopted by their grand-parents and the remaining five by their mothers and step-fathers. Interim orders could also have been appropriate in cases where doubts existed about the capacity of single applicants to cope on a long term basis with the demands of the adoption situation. (iv) To postpone the granting of the order: There were five such cases. One in order to give time to the applicants to improve their accommodation and in the remaining cases the court was awaiting for additional medical reports. (v) To refuse to make an order: The court may reach such a decision if it is not satisfied about the applicants' suitability or if it finds the natural parent's objection reasonable. There was only one case in which a court refused to grant an order in favour of grand-parents because the child's parents were not in agreement.

Varied Decision Making

Two types of adoption petitions appeared to cause anxieties to the courts. These were petitions by grand-parents (and occasionally by other relatives) and reclaims by the natural mothers.

(a) Petitions by grand-parents: It is quite clear that an application to adopt a grand-child or a related child is within the scope of the Adoption Act. The courts, however, appear to have no clear direction on the matter and so the practice varies from one area to another. In a well known case (re D.X - 1949, Ch. D. 320) Vaisey J, while urging caution in dealing with an application of this kind, pointed out that "every case must be judged on its own facts, dealt with on its own merits, and decided upon a balance of considerations"; he granted the order asked for, although the child's young mother was to remain under the same roof. Of orders made, 44 (or 4.7%) were in favour of grand-parents. In three quarters of these the children were illegitimate, and twenty of the natural mothers were still resident in the same household. The 20 courts in the sample took very varied attitudes to adoptions by grand-parents: two courts refused to accept such petitions; three others granted the orders but made a strong plea that the child's mother should move away from the same household and the child be told about his adoption; two other courts insisted on seeing the grand-parents before granting the petition and tried to impress on them the nature of adoption and the need to tell the child the truth about its parentage; the remaining 13 courts had no hesitation at all in granting such petitions.

In view of our earlier findings that some grand-parents do not tell the child about his true parentage, it may be thought that the granting of such orders involves a risk of possible psychological damage to the child. Others would argue, however, that the granting of the order in such cases merely sets a seal on a de facto adoption which would have continued in any event and which would have involved precisely the same risk. Some Sheriffs who follow the latter line, tend to believe that the risks are outweighed by the positive advantages of the child living with blood relatives. These advantages can be dubious, however, as seen from the following example: one case reported was that of a seven year old boy who was about to be adopted by his grand-parents, the only professional couple in this group of adoptions. The child was not aware of the true circumstances of his birth and the grand-parents were reticent about telling him the truth. They told the curator that the boy was subject to asthma and liable to suffer an attack when under strain or emotionally upset. After the grand-parents promised the curator that they would tell the child the truth about his parentage, the court proceeded to grant the order. Once the order is granted, there is no possibility of following up the case.

The motives behind such adoptions are unclear and their value is outweighed by some of the disadvantages we identified. Half the children were adopted when under two years old or three out of every four before they reached the age of five. This suggested some wish on the part of the grand-parents to regulate the child's circumstances before it came into contact with the outside world, such as school. A further explanation which suggested itself from some of the more informative reports, was that the grand-parents initiated adoption proceedings at a time when the child's mother was either about to marry or about to move away from the parental home. In both cases the mother's action appeared to trigger off a fear of loss in the grand-parents. In contrast to adoption by non-relatives, adoption by grand-parents, as well as by aunts and uncles, were mainly confined to the working classes. Adoption by grand-parents is a minority response but it has still to be proved whether they are sought by the less secure grand-parents.

(b) Reclaims by natural parent(s): These fall into two categories: Situations in which the parent withholds the original consent and situations in which the parent changes his mind after having signed an original consent.

(i) Withholding the consent: Situations of withholding original consent mostly arise in cases where the parent has disappeared

and cannot be found, or the parent turns up after a long dis-
appearance during which time the child was placed with a view
to adoption. Out of the sample of 1030 adoptions studied, original consents were not obtained from 21 parents (or 2.0%).
Eleven of these were mothers and 10 were "husbands of mothers".
Of the 11 mothers, 10 had disappeared and could not be found,
and the courts had no difficulty in dispensing with their consents. In the case of the one mother who appeared after a
period of long absence, a hearing was held and the mother's
consent was dispensed with for "persistently failing without
reasonable cause to discharge the obligation of a parent of
the infant". This was the only case in the sample in which a
Sheriff was asked to dispense with a consent according to the
new provisions of the 1958 Adoption Act. In the case of children whose parents have not officially surrendered them for adoption, but simply fail to carry out their parental obligations,
local authorities are very cautious in placing them for adoption. A number of such children are placed in long-term foster-
care with a possible view to adoption but some children may be
kept in nurseries for long periods in the hope that the parent(s)
may reappear. Because of the vagueness of the present provisions, local authorities and possibly adopters are reluctant
to take many risks whilst the child can remain in a state of
limbo. Even allowing for the new clause introduced in the
1958 Act, the court must still find that the parents are unreasonable in not giving their consent. But unreasonableness
has to be determined at the date of the hearing and not at any
other point of time (see re. L (an infant) 1962, 106, S.J. 611
and reported in the Times on the 19th July, 1962). In yet
another case, the Judge ruled that, if it is established that
the mother wants the child, that she is fit to be a mother,
and that she can support it, it is prima facie impossible to
say a decision not to have the child adopted is unreasonable.
(Ormerod L.J. In re. G. (an infant) 1965, 2 Q.B. 73 at p. 91).

The consent of the mother's husband to the adoption of
her extra-marital child is considered to be necessary. Ten
per cent of the children adopted were born to women whose
husbands were not the fathers of the children. The husbands
gave their consents in ninety per cent of these cases, and at
the suggestion of the curator, the courts dispensed with the
consent of the remaining husbands who could not be found.
The husbands who voluntarily signed their consents, did so to
facilitate the proceedings, though a few did so after the
curator promised to stress in his report that they were
signing as "husbands of the wife" and not as "fathers to the
child". In the case of husbands who could not be found, one
court expected the mother to sign an affidavit swearing to
non-access, but in all other cases the courts showed considerable flexibility by accepting the curator's recommendation.
The extent to which the curator pursued his enquiries depended on how well he was satisfied that there was no contact
between the mother and her husband during the period. We
came across no case where unnecessary anxiety or suffering

seemed to be invoked. The husbands in most cases were prepared to sign their consent and the mothers did not mind them knowing about this, as the marriage had been irretrievably broken down. In the few cases where husband and wife lived together, the circumstances were known to the husband.

(ii) <u>Change of mind by the natural parent</u>: The group of mothers who vacillate or who change their mind after signing their original consent, confront the court with a serious decision involving parental rights. The conflict at issue is the right of the parent to bring up his own child and the interests of the child to have an uninterrupted relationship with people it has already got to know and got attached to. The court, in considering whether the mother is unreasonable in <u>withdrawing</u> her consent, shall have regard to "the welfare of the infant". The fact, however, that a mother at first gives and subsequently withdraws consent is not per se evidence of unreasonableness, for this is a right granted to her by the Act, and its exercise is accordingly irrelevant to the question of unreasonableness. (See Jenkins Liv. in re. K (an infant) 1953, i Q.B. p. 117). Lord Denning, however, in re. L (an infant) 1962, 106 S.J. 611, added that "nevertheless, it is becoming increasingly clear that it may well be unreasonable for the parent to vacillate and so disregard the effect of her conduct upon the child and the adopters". In the whole of our court sample, we came across only seven cases (or 0.7%) in which the mother of a child changed her mind and asked for the child to be returned to her. Though this is a very tiny proportion compared to the total number of adoptions completed each year such cases can cause considerable misery and distress for everybody concerned. It is cases of this type that have led, over the last twenty years, to increased pressures to have the mother's consent made irrevocable at the time of surrender. Such proposals stem mainly from the wish to save the child from liability to the upsetting experiences of being moved after he has been in the prospective adopter's home for some months or years, and partly to save the adopters from the distress of having to part with the child to whom they have become attached. Dr. Soddy, [59] a psychiatrist, giving evidence in two cases where there was a possibility of transferring young infants under the age of 18 months, from one mother to another, summed up the views of child developmental experts by saying, "the effect of any change upon a child of his age (18 months) must be problematical, and I would say as a doctor that to move him would be to take an unjustifiable risk with his future".

The four courts which dealt with the seven cases of reclaims approached the matter in diverse ways. The varied decisions appeared to reflect personal beliefs rather than views derived from the psychosocial implications of each case. <u>Court No. 1</u>: Two cases came before this court of mothers who withheld confirmation of their consent and asked for their babies back. In both cases the court arranged for a full hearing at which all parties involved were separately heard. The first

mother maintained that when she was signing her consent, she
was not aware that it was irrevocable. The second mother had
changed her mind at least twice before. In both cases the
court found against the mothers for not being able to make
proper arrangements for the children. <u>Court No. 2</u>: The mother
of a two and a half years old boy refused to confirm her original consent. The child had been with the prospective adopters
for over two years but an application to adopt was delayed because of the mother's vacillation. The mother maintained at
the court that she was now in a position to take care of her
child. The court arranged to hear the mother only and after
doing so, it was satisfied that she was not unreasonable in
withholding her consent. Subsequently it asked the prospective adopters to return the child. There are reasonable doubts
as to whether "the welfare of the child" was considered, especially as neither the adopters nor the supervising authority
were heard by the court. The effect of the move to the child
was not considered. <u>Court No. 3</u>: This court received notification from the solicitors of two mothers intimating with-
drawal of their clients' consent and asking to have the
babies back. The children were six and four months old res-
pectively and had been with the prospective adopters almost
since birth. The court, without holding any kind of hearing,
directed the petitioners to return the children. The welfare
of the children was not apparently considered and the court
appeared to make an administrative decision in a dispute involving complex human relationships. <u>Court No. 4</u>: This
court dispensed with the consents of two mothers who refused
to confirm their original consents and wanted their children
back. Again, no hearing of any sort was held. One mother
told the curator that, when signing her original consent, she
was unaware that it was irrevocable, whilst the other claimed
that the adoption society, which arranged the placement, had
pointed out to her the possibility of court action by the
petitioners for compensation, if she refused to confirm her
consent. The court based its decision on the curators' reports, which indicated that both mothers had changed their
minds several times before.

Though all mothers who surrender through an agency are
furnished with an explanatory memorandum setting out the implications of their act, this point seems to merit further
consideration. There appears to be a strong case for more
reality to be injected into the whole process of signing away
one's child. The mothers are given the memorandum at a time
when they are in considerable distress and confusion and it
is arguable how much of its contents they take in. Furthermore, as the actual consent is usually given a few days or
weeks afterwards, there appears to be a separation of time
between the stage the memorandum is given to the mothers and
the signing of the consent.

<u>The dilemma of the court</u>: In cases where either of the par-
ents withholds his consent or changes his mind, the court
has to adjudicate on the issue of parental rights in the light

of the child's welfare. As the welfare of the child is such an intangible quality, it is not surprising that, over the years, courts have reached diverse decisions. The 'welfare' concept could be interpreted differently according to one's own views and especially how far studies in child development can influence the traditional 'blood tie' myth held by many judges. There is no neatly packaged, exhaustive judicial statement about the meaning of the child's welfare. Principles of material, physical and psychological, as well as spiritual welfare have all emerged from Scottish cases in the last twenty years. In Nicol V Nicol, 1953 S.L.T. (Notes) 67, the court took into account the living and other material conditions. In Barr V Barr, 1950 S.L.T. (Notes) 15, the court took into account such psychological factors as fear of living with a father. Some judges have also regarded it as undesirable to separate brothers and sisters: (Nicol v Nicol, supra). The most familiar case in matters of spiritual welfare is Mackay V Mackay, 1957 S.L.T. (Notes) 17 in which Lord President Clyde said: "Atheism and the child's welfare are almost necessarily mutually exclusive". In the same case Lord Carmont emphasised in somewhat broader terms that materialistic considerations are not the only ones.

The 1930 Adoption (Scotland) Act, declared with regard to adoption applications that "the order if made will be made for the welfare of the infant", but the subsequent Acts of 1950 and 1958, unlike the guardianship Act, strongly implied that the child's interests were not paramount. It has now been established beyond doubt that the test of reasonableness is not to be ascertained by reference to the interests of the child as the paramount consideration, as in custody cases, but by reference to the attitude of the mother. The welfare of the child is still subordinate to the legal rights of parents and it is the enforcement of these rights that often frustrates the adoption of a child. Mr. Justice Devlin, as he then was, is quoted as having made the following observation on the 1930 Act: "This gives an absolute discretion and in exercising their powers under a section so worded, the justices would no doubt be right in regarding as the matter of paramount importance the welfare of the child". He then went on to refer to the 1950 Act, and said: "However that may be, it is plain that the test is no longer the welfare of the child". (Reported in Child Adoption No. 53). The recent decision of the Court of Appeal (in Re. W (an infant) and reported in the Times of 14.5.70) demonstrated the almost total erosion of the 'welfare' concept. A mother aged 23 and unmarried, set up house with a man and had two daughters now aged five and four. She split up with that man and temporarily lived with another man, by whom she unintentionally conceived a boy who was the subject of the proposed adoption. The man left her when he found that she was pregnant. The child was born on March 28, 1968. Before the birth the mother was living in one room with the two girls. She felt that life with three small children would be impossible and made general arrangements for the adoption

of the boy before the birth. The boy, on April 5th, soon after
his birth, went to the proposed adopters as temporary foster-
parents and had remained with them ever since.   That arrangement was not with a view to adoption, but they became attached
to the child, and in September, 1968, they indicated to the
local authority that they wished to adopt him.   The mother
signed the appropriate statutory consent form on February, 11th
1969 and the hearing of the adoption proceedings was fixed for
April 1st.   On March 30th, however, the mother wrote with-
drawing her consent.   The judge expressed himself as satisfied
that the mother's consent was being unreasonably withheld and
decided to dispense with her consent and make the adoption
order.   The mother appealed on the ground that she had not
unreasonably withheld her consent.

The Court of Appeal which was composed of Lord Justice
Russell, Lord Justice Sachs and Lord Justice Cross delivered
a judgement on 13.5.70.   It declared that an unmarried mother
who withholds her consent to the adoption of her child is not
being unreasonable in doing so although the child's future
prospects may be better with the proposed adoptive parents, as
the child's welfare is not the paramount consideration as it
is in custody proceedings.   Only very special circumstances
can justify the permanent severance by adoption of the natural bond between mother and child against the mother's wishes.

This latest decision, following that reached in the now
famous 'blodd tie' case in 1965, polarises further the feelings
between those who believe in the importance of maintaining
the 'blood tie' or the 'natural bond' and those who see emotional attachment as more important.   When a state like this is
reached, it is time for the legislators to take a more defin-
-ite stand.   There is need for a clearer direction in the
matter lest an increasing number of children are exposed to
unnecessary emotional hazards and even to the permanent lack
of a stable home.   A further difficulty is that in such disputed cases, the Adoption Act makes no provision about what
should be done with the child in the meantime.

A complication which has contributed further to the erosion of the child's welfare, is the conflicting provisons
of the Adoption Act of 1958 and the Legitimacy Act of 1959.
Though the father of an illegitimate child is not a parent,
within the meaning of the Adoption Act, under sec. 3 of the
1959 Legitimacy Act, he has a right to initiate proceedings
for the custody of his child.   This right enables a father to
delay or even prevent the making of an adoption order.
Furthermore, whether the father's right to be heard, under
the Adoption Act, involves also a right to be notified of
the hearing and whether the curator should seek him out, or
do so only if he has maintained an interest in the child,
are matters over which there is no agreement among the courts.
The most well-known case, which illustrates the conflict between the two Acts quoted above, is what has come to be known
as the 'blood-tie' case.   The gist of the case is that a baby

boy was born out-of-wedlock to a single girl in July, 1964. The
father was a married man, whose first marriage had ended in
divorce, and who was at the time estranged from his second
wife. The affair between him and the mother of the child
started in April, 1963. In August, 1963 the father and the
mother intended to marry and were waiting for the outcome of
the divorce proceedings started by the father's second wife.
After the mother became pregnant with this child, she told the
father that she was not interested in marrying him any longer,
but she did not tell him that she was expecting. After the
child was born, the mother approached an adoption society and
arranged to place the child for adoption. The father, who came
to know about this, approached the society and tried to verify
this, but the society refused to discuss the matter with him.
On 31.8.64 the child was handed over to prospective adopters,
but on 14.9 of the same year, the father took out a summons
for custody under the Legitimacy Act of 1959. Proceedings
for the adoption were stayed until the custody application
was heard. In the meantime, the father was reconciled with
his second wife and went to live with her. It was not until
15.12.65 that the case came before the High Court of Appeal.
By this time the child had been with the prospective adopters
for over 18 months.

The Appeal Court reached its decision by a majority
vote and found in favour of the father. The High Court Judge
referred to the "blood relationship" between the father and
the child, and what he described as "instinctual bond" between
them. The Judge concluded, "There is a risk, but it seems to
me the prize is something which cannot otherwise be had for
this child, that he should know who he is and be brought up
by his own people". The evidence of a child psychiatrist outlining the possible risks to the child's future emotional
well-being were set aside. In their judgement, the concurring
judges lumped together two separate things; i.e. knowledge
about who one is, and being brought up by one's own people.
The first, which appears to be the most important, an adopted
person can obtain through his adoptive parents, unless the
latter fail to share such vital information with him.

All judges involved in this case rightly criticised
strongly the adoption society for proceeding to place the
child with adopters, though it knew that this was a disputed
case. Again, however, as neither the Adoption Act or the
Legitimacy Act make any provision about what should be done
with the child in the meantime, it can only be assumed that
the child would have to go to a residential nursery or to a
temporary foster home. The long time that it took both courts
to reach their decision, would have left the children in a
limbo state with considerable adverse effects to their mental
health.

Lord Denning in re "O" an infant (1965) Chancery Division, page 23, at page 28, expressed a different view about the
position of a putative father, when, he said: "The natural

father is not in the same position as a legitimate father. He
is a person who is entitled to special consideration by the tie
of blood, but not to any greater or other right. His father-
hood is a ground to which regard should be paid in seeing what
is best <u>in the interests of the child</u>, but it is not an over-
riding consideration".

The conflicting provisions of the two Acts has, to a certain extent led to a reluctance in some agencies to involve the
putative father, for fear he might decide to take action for
custody under the Legitimacy Act. In the whole of our sample,
however, we came across only one case where the natural father
of a child objected to the making of an order. He did not
take custody proceedings and though the court gave him the
opportunity to be heard, he failed to turn up. His consent was
subsequently dispensed with.

Length of Time Between Application and the Making of the Order.

One in every five orders were granted within the first
four weeks following the submission of the petition; one in
every four took between five and eight weeks, a similar number
were granted between nine to 13 weeks, whilst the remainder
were delayed beyond three months. In all, seven out of every
ten orders were granted within the first three months. The average
age time between the placement of the child and the granting of
the order was six and a half months and the average time between the submission of the petition and the granting of the
order was just under three months.

The granting of adoption orders could be speeded up if:
(i) placing agencies were to submit the petitions without
waiting for the expiry of the three months probationary period;
(ii) social workers, when acting as curators, could speed up
the preparation of their reports; (iii) a number of Sheriff
courts could speed up the appointment of the curator; and (iv)
some Sheriff courts could speed up the disposal of the applications.

Conclusions

The study showed that the function of the curator, as
currently performed, fails in most cases to meet the objectives set out by the regulations. Similarly, Sheriff courts
granted the vast majority of the orders in an impersonal administrative way and only in a tiny number of disputed cases did
the Sheriffs involve themselves in some real decision making.
The various courts reached widely differing decisions when
issues concerning the child's welfare were at stake. The need
for clarification in this area seems overdue.

CHAPTER   TWELVE

FINAL CONCLUSIONS AND DISCUSSION

        This study set out to identify current adoption practice
in Scotland and to evaluate it in the light of standards developed by the social work profession and those set up by the law.
Any study that involves an evaluative approach of this type
cannot entirely **escape** the criticism of some element of subjectivity. No accurate methods have as yet been developed to
make it possible for one human being to measure the work of
another in matters involving complex human situations. We
would like to feel that the safeguards built into this study
lessened the danger of subjective judgement. If the findings
appear to be critical of the practitioner, it is not because of
bias in the analysis which reflected, as accurately as possible,
the content of the records available. It is very possible that
important material was not recorded and therefore could not be
evaluated. So little is known about the outcome of adoption
and of the different practices used, that to stress the need
for detailed recording, which could help to identify what is
useful and what can be discarded, is like stating the obvious.
Preliminary observations since the end of this study in 1968,
indicate that some improvement has been taking place. Some
agencies have been appointing trained staff and giving more
thought to their practices. The thought-out practices of a
minority of agencies are now beginning to stimulate wider
interest.

        The overall conclusion is that, with some very interest-
ing exceptions, adoption practice was found to be based on an
extremely narrow range of tangible and repetitive factors.
The range of observations, thought and action was very limited
compared to social work expectations and the respective merit
of a range of possible activities were not considered. It
would be unfair, however, to underestimate the complexities of
adoption practice, and unjustifiable to ascribe other than the
best of motives to those charged with the responsibility of
bringing about the child/parent relationship, without the
necessary training and resources. These deficiencies may
partly account too, for the failure of almost all agencies to
formulate their practice into a body of working principles,
and then regularly to re-examine and review these principles
and the methods used, in order to ensure the best possible
service to all parties participating in the adoption situation.
Instead, to a large extent the general approach to the work
was amateurish and aimed only at meeting legal and administrative requirements, failing to take into account the complexity of the human situations involved. Assessments were
mostly based on intuition or even whims and did not reflect any
organised body of knowledge or any discernible method. The
work with the natural parents, the child and the adopters, bore
little relation to the standards recommended by the social work

profession. Many aspects of the practice, such as a blanket
type of practice for all clients, were a negation of basic
social work principles about the individuality of every human
situation; similarly there was lack of conviction about the
basic concepts of child welfare such as the beneficial effect
of environmental influences and the reversibility of certain
experiences. A biologistic determinism was identifiable in
many aspects of the practice. In spite of reassurances in
social work literature and in official documents that adoption
is now practised mainly in the interests of the child, the
study came across considerable evidence suggesting that the
attitudes of various individuals responsible for bringing about the child/parent relationship were largely adoptive-
parent orientated and seldom child-centred. A further observation was the tendency of almost all agencies to elevate
certain legal requirements into practice principles and transfer them to non-relevant situations. For instance, the legal
requirement that no mother can give her written consent before
the baby is six weeks' old, was built into a practice principle
requiring that no child be placed or be medically examined
before it is six weeks's old; or that all children need a
six weeks' pre-adoption placement.

The multiplicity of individuals and bodies involved in
the adoption process, far from safeguarding the child's welfare, served to create a false sense of security. Each one of
these agents or agencies i.e. the placing agency, the supervising officer, the curator ad litem and the Sheriff, acted
independently and in isolation from each other. Too much
seemed to be assumed that was not justified by actual events.
Each successive person involved, for instance, assumed that
the previous one or the one about to come had carried or
would carry out certain investigations or offer certain services. The present function of such agents as supervising
officers, curators and even Sheriffs could be dispensed with
and replaced by fewer and perhaps more effective agents that
could ensure that certain services are offered or certain investigations are carried out at the stage most vital in the proceedings.

It is recognised that no amount of legislation can improve
some of the practices found in the course of this study and, in
fact, legislation now advocated around certain areas, such as
rapid termination of parental rights, would be seen as premature without a corresponding improvement in agency practices.
The study indicates that most of the changes need to come from
within the placing agencies themselves. To do this, they will
need more resources to help them to employ trained workers and
to develop programmes with wider objectives. It will in fact
be a great advance when services to unmarried mothers in general and adoption services come to be offered within the same
agencies, instead of the present fragmented set up which fails
to ensure proper coverage.

The greatest challenge facing adoption practice, as it

emerged from the study, is the need for a change of those attitudes based on preconceived or out-dated beliefs and prejudices,
and a shift away from amateurism and traditionalism so that
adoption work may be brought into line with modern concepts of
child welfare. Traditional attitudes, reflecting the desire to
place 'perfect' babies, or match by socio-economic background,
die hard, but the emerging need is for new policies and attitudes that can promote the needs of "hard-to-place" children.
The study has also found a gradual drop in the number of applicants coming forward to adopt and this may not be entirely un-
connected with the unwholesome image that some adoption agencies have projected of themselves. The rejection of applicants
hitherto on the basis of single factors of doubtful validity,
has not been much of an encouragement to new applicants. For a
sense of fairness to prevail, greater honesty on the part of
agencies will be needed and a start could be made by making
their eligibility and other criteria public. The present in-
appropriate secrecy appears to serve the needs of the organ-
isation rather than those of the community. It contrasts
sharply with the advice adoption workers give to adoptive parents, to be honest with the child.

Specific Areas for Legal Changes

Three of the key figures in the adoption process, i.e.
the supervising officer, the curator and the Sheriff, lacked
conviction about the importance of their role and acted simply
in a routine way to satisfy administrative and legal requirements. All three appeared to come into the adoption situation
too late to be of any practical help, and so they tended to
sanction the placing practices of the various agencies. The
study has identified the need for improved agency practices
and for administrative and legal changes aimed at limiting
the number of persons and agencies involved in the adoption
process.

Adoption societies and local authority agencies: The present
regulations providing for the registration of adoption societies afford only formal control over their work. Adoption
societies are at the moment entrusted with a great amount of
authority and responsibility with very little accountability
for their practices. This is giving increasing concern to
the public. The varying practices identified in the course
of this study, far from suggesting strength arising out of
diversity, were mainly the result of personal beliefs and of
ad hoc and piecemeal considerations, rather than of well
thought out principles and concepts reflecting current knowledge and thinking on the subject. Because local authorities were mainly found to run their own adoption services on
similar and sometimes on less effective lines, they did not
seem to be the right bodies to undertake the responsibility
of acting either as registering or as 'inspecting' authorities. Changes in the law that would, directly or indirectly,
bestow more authority on adoption agencies without corresponding accountability, would, in the light of these findings, be considered as premature and perhaps not in the

best interests of the parties involved in the adoption situation.

Voluntary societies were found to be operating under conditions of extreme financial difficulty and some explicit provision for local authority grants to be made available to them
could help to provide badly needed improvements, and more important, to widen their programmes. Our argument for local
authority grants is strengthened by the fact that a number of
the new social work departments are delegating their adoption
work to voluntary societies. Grants could help societies to
employ trained staff, though such staff are unlikely to be
attracted unless committess are prepared to relinquish a considerable amount of control. The law could help in this respect by defining more precisely what is meant by a 'fit' person to be employed in an adoption agency and also by clarify-
ing the boundaries between the role of the case committee and
that of its professionals. Individual case decisions, being
professional matters, should be left to the deliberations of
professionals from within the agency, assisted by co-opted advisors from other allied disciplines. Because of the variety
of eligibility criteria used, agencies should be required to
make these public, not only for applicants to know where they
stand, but also to make these open to public scrutiny and discussion.

Unlike the present system local authority agencies should
be subject to the same regulations as voluntary ones. The absence of explicit regulations controlling the adoption work of
local authorities gives the impression of different standards
required of the two types of agencies, and it may have contributed to the overall 'poor' quality of the practices found including the failure to collect elementary statistics and often
quite basic information.

The law could help to generate some new thinking about the
needs of "hard-to-place" children, who are not accommodated
within the narrow programmes of most agencies. As a first
step, the Act may have to give powers to local authorities to
subsidise, where appropriate, certain types of guardianship
adoptions. Similarly, more effective ways will have to be
found to make possible the adoption of children who are now in
long term care and whose parents lose interest in them, the
children remaining in a state of limbo. The delicate problem
of balancing the welfare of the child with the rights of the
parents seems to need a totally new approach. The provisions
of the existing Act have proved inadequate for the purpose.

Medical certificates: The practice of obtaining medical certificates on adopters after the placement, offers no protection
to the child. It is important that the applicants' health is
considered at the selection stage and that a less rigid and
more informative medical certificate reaches both the placing
agency and the court.

The Mother's consent: The giving or withholding of consents by

the natural mother is tied up with the child's welfare. The
cases quoted in chapter eleven highlighted contrasting court
decisions and pointed to the urgent need for clarification of
the 'welfare' concept. As many courts appear to disregard the
accumulated evidence from studies of child development, more
definite direction may have to come from the legislators. Any
decisions will inevitably have to balance the rights of the
natural mother with those of the child. This could be reached
by taking into account both the insights gained from studies
of child development, as well as the timing of the mother's
decision regarding adoption and her attitude to the timing
and finality of consents. No study is as yet available about
the mother's attitude to the timing and finality of consents,
but existing studies suggest that between seventy and eighty
per cent of single mothers reach a final decision about their
child within seven to ten days after confinement. It would be
reasonable, therefore, to provide for the mother's consent to
be given at an earlier stage than the present six weeks statutory requirement. The possibility of an earlier consent
would offer the mother the opportunity to change her mind when
the child is about to be placed or before it has spent too
much time with the adopters. If provision is made for the
original consent to be given earlier, it would be reasonable
to make it final within a specified time-span. Any such
change, however, must be preceded by measures aiming at ensuring far more reality than at present to be injected into
the surrendering process and the actual signing of the consent.
This study has shown that most mothers had only a perfunctory
contact with the adoption worker and only a minority of
agencies offered a personal casework service with opportunities to discuss alternatives to adoption. The study has also
come across a few disquieting cases where it appeared that
mothers were unnecessarily hurried or misled about their exact
rights and obligations. Any change aimed at terminating parental rights at an earlier stage, without first ensuring substantial improvement in agency practice, would be premature
and a step in the wrong direction. These and other important
reasons would also argue against a provision to surrender the
child to the agency instead of the adopters.

Third party placements: The very small number of third party
placements found in this study, do not suggest any drastic
change is needed in this area. No evidence was found to
support allegations of illicit traffic in babies and anxieties
about third party adoptions appear to have been over-exaggerated.
The main argument against third party adoptions is that the
adopters are not properly selected, the natural parents get no
casework help and the child is not properly assessed. All
three arguments are demolished by our findings which showed
that, in the majority of agency placements, the adoptive parents
were not better selected, the natural parents received no
casework help and the child's assessment amounted only to a
formal medical examination to satisfy certain requirements. As
long as the decisions of most agencies are based on a narrow
range of criteria, such as those found in the study, the

consumer needs some protection, whilst care is taken to safeguard the interests of the child. Our subsequent suggestion to
make all placements notifiable to the courts in advance, should
act as a safeguard against possible abuses of the system by
third party agents.

Statutory supervision: The nature of statutory supervision, as
currently practised, seems to offer only minimum protection to
the child and is of no perceptible value to the adopters. If,
however, our earlier suggestion for an improvement of voluntary agency practices, is brought about, there will then be no
obvious reason why the placing agencies should not carry out
post-placement supervision. A greater scrutiny of the practices
of all types of placing agencies could ensure a more satisfactory type of post-placement supervision, without it being
necessary to introduce a statutory form of supervision. Statutory supervision should be reserved for all independent placings, provided again that this type of work does not continue
to be seen as the cinderella among the agencies' case-loads.
A duty should be placed on placing agencies to provide the
courts with social reports setting out the circumstances of
the contemplated adoption.

The curator ad litem: The study showed that the function of
the curator, as currently performed, failed in most cases to
meet the objectives set out in the regulations. The findings
point to two possible changes: one to abolish this role altogether and strengthen the part played by the supervising
officer, or to strengthen the role of the curator. If the
latter suggestion is adopted, it would be in the best interests
of the child, those of his parents and of the adopters, if
placing agencies and others arranging adoptions independently,
were required to give advance notice to the court of their intention to place a child. The curator, who should be a highly
skilled social worker, should then carry out the appropriate
investigations and report his findings to the court; the latter
could then proceed to approve or reject the proposed placement
depending on the reported circumstanced. This would not only
go a long way to safeguard the child's welfare, but would also
make the work of the curator and the courts appear less futile
and pointless than at present. This process, however, would
need very speedy action as adoption work is a race against
time. Such an initial investigation would be in addition to
the subsequent formal hearing when the supervising or placing
agency should play the predominant role in furnishing reports
etc. It is also imperative that the law clarifies what is
the precise status of the confidential report of the curator.

The Sheriff: The Sheriff courts are now mainly engaged in making routine administrative decisions based on a very limited
range of factors. Adoption work is only a fringe activity of
these courts and, with the new provision for children's cases
to be brought before Children's Hearings, it would be an
anachronism to leave this type of work within the Sheriff
Court with its quasi-criminal function. Though nobody yet

knows how these Hearings will work out in practice, it is
hoped that with their constant interaction with social agencies
and with family problems and situations, they will develop considerable knowledge and expertise in handling complex problems
involving social and psychological factors. Provisions for a
court hearing, however, would have to be arranged for cases
where disputes about parental rights arose.

Adoptions by relatives: Any change in the law cannot fail to
look again at the implications arising out of the adoption of
legitimate and illegitimate children by their mothers and their
husbands, as well as by their grand-parents and other relatives.
The advantages that such adoptions confer on the children are
questionable, whilst, on the other hand, they were found, in
some cases, to encourage secrecy and evasiveness which did not
appear to be in the best interests of the child.

Duty of local authorities: In view of the findings which suggest
that there is a close association between adoption numbers and
availability of opportunity to surrender or to adopt, and that
where there are such opportunities third party adoptions are
few, there are good reasons why a duty should be placed on
local authorities to provide adoption services and services to
unmarried mothers in general. An explicit responsibility on
local authorities to provide such services may help to generate more interest and thinking, especially as regards long
term care and the cases of children who are often considered
as 'unadoptable'.

Final Conclusion

     Society is constantly undergoing changes and, as adoption
practice has formerly been affected by changing attitudes and
beliefs, as well as by knowledge from the scientific field,
future changes may have similar effects. Because adoption is
an institution which does not exist in a void, it is essential
for the practitioner to develop a frame of mind geared towards change. The survival of practice, and whether it continues to lie in the hands of social workers, may be dependent
on how far the latter are prepared to look critically at their
work, to view new concepts with an open mind and be ready to
try innovations and use findings from research studies. A
failure to develop in these ways may result either in the
agencies disappearing because of failure to adapt or in the
public turning away from practices that appear to be becoming
fossilised.

                              II

Current Studies

     The main study suggested a number of specific areas where
further research would be needed to provide information on
certain processes and situations. As a result the following
studies have been initiated and are now in progress:

(i) <u>The timing of the mothers' decision regarding adoption and</u>
<u>their attitudes to the legal/administrative process of adoption,</u>
<u>and in particular to the timing and finality of consents.</u>

The aim of this study is to provide evidence which can be
used by the Departmental Committee on Adoption (which has
commissioned the study) in considering whether changes should
be made in the arrangements by which natural mothers give consent to adoption. A case study is being made of one group of
approximately 70 mothers who are being confined in Edinburgh
hospitals. The mothers will be interviewed twice, first
shortly after confinement and before leaving hospital and
again soon after the adoption is granted. Some of the questions the study hopes to answer are: (a) When do most mothers
who part with their babies make a firm decision for adoption?
(b) When do they want consent to be final, and is this influenced by whether or not they have experienced separation
from their child before it is placed with adopters? (c) Is
the minimum period of six weeks before consent relevant to
most mothers' wishes?

A similar study is also simultaneously being carried out
in two separate centres in England under the auspices of the
British Association of Adoption Societies.

(ii) <u>Adopted adults who enquire about their natural parents.</u>

Under the provisions of the Adoption Act 1958, the
Registrar-General maintains an Adopted Children's Register in
which entries are made following every adoption order. He
also keeps an index of the Adopted Children's Register which
is open to public search. In addition, however, he keeps a
register of births which makes traceable the connection between an entry in the register of births which had been
marked "adopted" and any corresponding entry in the Adopted
Children's Register. In England and Wales such registers are
not open to inspection or search "except under an order of a
Court...", but the Scottish Adoption Act provides that information from this Register can be made available to the
adopted persons themselves after they have attained the age
of 17 years. The provisions of the Scottish Adoption Act
offer a unique opportunity to find out more about the tiny
number of people (approximately fifty each year) who ask for
information about their natural parent(s).

In the study we plan to interview approximately fifty
adopted adults who enquire at the Registrar-General's Office
and who volunteer to participate in the project. The aim of
the study is to provide information about the circumstances
that prompted these people to find out more about their
origin; how they came to know about this opportunity; the
use they made of the information gained; their reaction to
it; and their general views about the amount of information
desirable and how best it can be made available. In the
last twenty or so years several writers have stressed how important it is for adopted persons to receive as much

information as possible about their origin. This, it is claimed, would strengthen the adopted person's sense of identity and contribute to his general mental well-being. Adoptive parents are now urged to tell children about their adoption and to share relevant background information with them.

(iii) One of the biggest challenges facing adoption practice to-day is the problem of the 'hard-to-place' child. No information is available at the moment about the number of children who, for a variety of reasons, have been refused adoption. A pilot study was therefore initiated in one local authority department to test the hypothesis that 'a considerable number of children are not placed for adoption either because of a handicap (medical, age or colour) or because of the lack of agency time to attend to their needs'. The study aims at identifying and examining the reasons and circumstances that prevented these children from being placed. If the pilot study substantiates the hypothesis, it will be followed by a wider study based on a national sample.

BIBLIOGRAPHY

1. Forster, F.S. "Isaeus", Heinman, London, 1927.

2. Mead, M "Coming of Age in Samoa", Pelican, London, 1966; also "Growing up in New Guinea", Pelican, London, 1954.

3. Crammond, W. "Illegitimacy in Banffshire", Banff, 1888.

4. Letters from Lady M.W. Montagu 1709-1762 "Everyman's Library, London, 1925 Vol.I p. 170.

5. Gerin, W. "Charlotte Bronte", Oxford Clarendon Press, 1967, p.165.

6. Elliott, G. "Silas Marner" The Thames Publishing Co. London, p.159.

7. Anderson, W. "Children Rescued from Pauperism or the Boarding-Out System", Edinburgh, 1871.

8. J.J. Henley "Report of J.J. Henley Poor Law Inspector to the Poor Law Board, on the Boarding-Out of Pauper Children in Scotland" HMSO 1870.

9. "Protection of Infant Life" H.M.S.O. p.372, 1871.

10. Memorandum..... on the 1908 Children's Act Glasgow Parish Council, 1911.

11. Best, H. "The War Baby" Stanley Paul & Co., London, 1915.

12. Report of the Committee on Child Adoption, Cmd, 1254, 1921.

13. Child Adoption Committee, First Report, Cmd 2401, 1925, Second Report, Cmd 2469, 1926; Third Report, Cmd 2711, 1926.

14. Browne, M. "How far public opinion has moved in a more liberal direction with regard to illegitimacy in the past twenty years" - Privately circulated paper (1965).

15. Hamilton, M. "Extra-marital conception in adolescence", Brit. Journal of Psychiatric Social Work, Vol. 6, No. 13, 1962.

16. Report of the Departmental Committee on Adoption Societies and Agencies, H.M.S.O. cmd 5499, 1936.

17. Report of the Departmental Committee on the Adoption of Children", Chaired by Sir Gerald Hurst, H.M.S.O. Cmd 9248, 1954.

18. R.A. Parker "Research in Adoption" Case Conference Sept. 1963 pp95 - 100.

19. C.E. Vincent "Illegitimacy in the next Decade: Trends and Implications" Child Welfare, Vol. XLIII, No. 10, Dec. 1964 pp.513-521.

20. M.L. Kelmer Pringle "Adoption - Facts and Fallacies", Longmans 1967.

21. H.J. Meyer, W. Jones and E.F. Borgatta "The Decision by Unmarried Mothers to keep or Surrender their Babies", Social Work, XIII, April, 1956 pp.103 - 9.

22. M.A. Yelloly "Factors Relating to an Adoption Decision by the Mothers of Illegitimate Infants", The Sociological Review Vol. 13, No. 1, March, 1965, pp.5 - 14.

23. J.P. Triseliotis "The Timing of the Single Mother's Decision in Relation to Agency Practice" - Child Adoption, No. 58, October, 1969.

24. D.G. Gill "Illegitimacy and Adoption: Its Socio-economic Correlates. A Preliminary Report". Child Adoption, No.56, No. 1 of 1969 pp.25 - 37.

25. C.E. Vincent, J.S. Pearson and P.S. Amacher "Intellectual Testing Results and Observations of Personality Disorder among 3594 Unwed Mothers in Minnesota" Journal of Clinical Psychology, XII, No. 1, Jan. 1956 pp.16 - 21.

26. L. Young "Out of Wedlock", McGraw Paperbacks, New York, 1954.

27. C.E. Vincent "Unmarried Mothers" Free Press of Glencoe, N/York, 1961.

28. H.R. Wright "80 Unmarried Mothers Who Kept thier Babies" Dept. of Social Welfare, State of California (1965).

29. D. Levy "A follow-up study of unmarried mothers" Social Casework XXXVI, 1955, pp.27 - 33.

30. M. Nott "Breaking Adoption Bottlenecks" Survey, October, 1950.

31. "Workloads in Children's Departments" H.M.S.O., SBN11 - 340101 - 9 (1969).

32. "Report of the Conference Held at Folkestone", October, 1961, SCSRA.

33. J. Rowe "Parents Children and Adoption", RKP, London, 1966.

34. J. Nicholson "Mother and Baby Homes" Allen and Unwin, London, 1968.

35. J.O. Forfar "Worth and Need in Medico-Social Assessment: the Adoption Situation" Child Adoption, 57 of 1969 pp.25-33.

36. M.A. Ribble "The Rights of Infants" Columbia Univ. Press, 1943.

37. "Standards for Adoption Service" Child Welfare League of America, Inc. 1958 and 1965.

38. S. Karelitz "Paediatrics and Adoption" in Schapiro (ed.) "A Study of Adoption Practice", Vol.II, 1956.

39. J. Bowlby "Child Care and the Growth of Love", Pelican, London, 1953, p.122.

40. Witmer, H.L., Herzog, E., Weinstein, E.A. & Sullivan, M.E., "Independent Adoptions - A follow-up study", Russell Sage Foundation, N/York, 1963.

41. H.S. Maas "The Successful Adoptive Parent Applicant" Social Work, 5 pp.14 - 20. Jan., 1960.

42. J.H. Reid "Principles, Values and Assumptions Underlying Adoption Practice" Social Work, Vol.2, No.1 (1957).

43. C.S. Amatruda and J.V. Baldwin "Current Adoption Practices", Journal of Paediatrics, 38, p.208 - 12 (1951).

44. J.R. Wittenborn "The Placement of Adoptive Children", Springfield, Illinois, U.S.A., (1957).

45. R.F. Brenner "A Follow-up Study of Adoptive Families" Child Adoption Research Committee, N/York (1951).

46. R.J. Goldman "A critical and historical survey of the methods of child adoption in the U.K. and the U.S.A." - M.A. thesis Birmingham University, 1958.

47. M. Kornitzer "Adoption and Family Life", Putman, London (1968).

48. D. Gough "Problems of Adoption", Almoner pp.110-112 (1959).

49. M. Humphrey and C. Ounsted "Adoptive Families Referred for Psychiatric Advice: Part II. The Parents", Brit. Journal of Psychiatry, 110, pp.549-55 (1964).

50. H.D. Kirk "Shared Fate" The Free Press of Glencoe, London, 1964.

51. L. Ripple "A follow-up Study of Adopted Children" Social Service Review Dec. 1968, pp.479-99.

52. R. Steinman "How Important is likeness in Adoption?" Child Welfare XXXII, No. 8, October, 1953.

53. M. Davis and P. Bouck "Crucial Importance of Adoption Home Study", Child Welfare Vol. XXXIV No.3, March 1955, pp.20-21.

54. M.B. Loe "Prediction - A Realistic Aspect of Adoption Practice", in M. Schapiro (ed.) "A Study of Adoption Practice", Vol.II, 1956.

55. M. Skodak and H. Skeels "A Final Follow-up Study of One Hundred Adopted Children", Jour. of Genetic Psychology, 75, 1949.

56. M. Humphrey and C. Ounsted "Adoptive Families Referred for Psychiatric Advice: Part I: The Children". Brit. Jour. of Psychiatry, 109, pp.599 - 608 (1963).

57. D. Jehu "Developmental issues in interracial adoption" S.C.S.R.A., 1968.

58. L. Blom-Cooper "Parental Rights in Adoption Cases", Child Adoption, 56, No. 1, 1969.

59. K. Soddy (In the matter of C - an infant - in the High Court of Justice 15.12.65).